I0796549

BROKEN ARROW

REEL WEST

ANDREW PATRICK NELSON, SERIES EDITOR

Reel West is a unique series of short, neatly packaged volumes exploring individual Western films across the whole history of the canon, from early and classic Westerns to revisionist and neo-Westerns. The series considers the many themes and variations that have accrued over more than a century of this most American of film styles. Intended for general readers as well as for classroom use, these brief books offer smart, incisive examinations of the aesthetic, cultural, experiential, and personal meaning and legacy of the films they discuss and provide strong arguments for their importance—all filtered through the consciousness of writers of distinction from within the disciplines of film history, journalism, and literature.

Also available in the Reel West Series:

The Man Who Shot Liberty Valance by Chris Yogerst
Ride the High Country by Robert Nott
Thelma & Louise by Susan Kollin
Ride Lonesome by Kirk Ellis
Blood on the Moon by Alan K. Rode

BROKEN ARROW

ANGELA ALEISS

University of New Mexico Press | Albuquerque

Printed in the United States of America

ISBN 978-0-8263-6832-4 (paper)
ISBN 978-0-8263-6833-1 (ePub)

Library of Congress Control Number: 2025006425

Founded in 1889, the University of New Mexico sits on the traditional homelands of the Pueblo of Sandia. The original peoples of New Mexico—Pueblo, Navajo, and Apache—since time immemorial have deep connections to the land and have made significant contributions to the broader community statewide. We honor the land itself and those who remain stewards of this land throughout the generations and also acknowledge our committed relationship to Indigenous peoples. We gratefully recognize our history.

Cover illustration: still from *Broken Arrow*
Designed by Felicia Cedillos
Composed in Adobe Jenson Pro

Dedicated to Delmer, Mary Lou, and Michael Daves

CONTENTS

ACKNOWLEDGMENTS

I would like to acknowledge the following individuals and institutions for their help with this manuscript: Howard Prouty and Tony Guzman, Margaret Herrick Library, Academy of Motion Picture Arts and Sciences; Martin Gostanian, the Paley Center for Media; the late Ned Comstock, University of Southern California, Cinematic Arts Library; Sally Newland, Amerind Museum; Doug Hocking, author of *Tom Jeffords: Friend of Cochise*; Marc Wanamaker, Bison Archives; and Roger Leatherwood, UCLA Instructional Media Library.

I would also like to thank Kathy Klump, Chiricahua Regional Museum and Research Center; Major Darren Johnson, Military Academy at West Point; David Gonzales, Stanford Alumni Association; Robert N. Watt, University of Birmingham, UK; David A. Olson, Columbia Rare Book & Manuscript Library; the staff at the American Heritage Center, University of Wyoming; Erin Fehr, Sequoyah National Research Center, University of Arkansas at Little Rock; John Belton, Rutgers University; Maggie Dwenger, Special Collections, University of Arizona Libraries; and Thomas Doherty, Brandeis University. I am especially grateful to Luana Ross (Confederated Salish and Kootenai Tribes), University of Washington.

I extend a special thanks to Andrew Patrick Nelson, editor of the Reel West series, and Stephen Hull at the University of New Mexico Press.

Finally, I am especially grateful to Fred Clark, former director of the Office of Tribal Relations, US Forest Service, as well as the following tribal communities who assisted me with preparation of this manuscript: the San Carlos Apache and White Mountain Apache Tribe of Arizona, the Mescalero Apache Tribe of New Mexico, and the Modoc Nation and the Fort Sill Apache Tribe of Oklahoma.

Introduction

Stories of the Apache chief Cochise have fascinated filmmakers and other artists for over one hundred years. One of them was Delmer Daves, who chose the remarkable friendship between Cochise and the US mail rider Thomas Jeffords as the subject for his first Western, *Broken Arrow* (1950).

My fascination with *Broken Arrow* began decades ago when I met Daves at a seminar in San Diego. He was close to seventy years old at the time, with a kindly demeanor and a booming voice that easily commanded attention. As a feature of the seminar, Daves screened his later Western *Cowboy* (1958), a film about a rugged cattle drive starring Glenn Ford and Jack Lemmon. But Daves's discussion of *Broken Arrow* and its Apaches captivated me. As a native of the Valentine State—so named because it joined the Union on February 14, 1912—I became fascinated with Arizona history. The actual *Broken Arrow* story took place deep within the rugged Dragoon Mountains in southeastern Arizona, which I visited several times as a volunteer for the US Forest Service Tribal Relations.

Daves, however, chose to set the Cochise/Jeffords's story against the stunning backdrop of Sedona, Arizona. The region lies three hundred miles north of the Dragoons and has nothing to do with Chiricahua history. Still, Sedona's picturesque red-rock buttes and steep canyon walls provided an ideal setting for the director's vision of Arizona's Anglo-Apache history, with its interracial romance and a "permanent" peace between whites and Apaches.[1] Alas, neither event is historically true.

Years later, I had several discussions with Daves's son Michael, who invited me to his late father's home in Los Angeles. Delmer's house was a trove of literature and artwork from his extensive travels around the world. Michael, who had inherited his father's wanderlust, became an assistant director, and he too shuttled between his home in Los Angeles and various far-flung locations. "It's hard to keep a marriage together when you're always on the road," he told me. "But I love my work. There's nothing else I would rather do." Michael's recollections of his father were essential for my article, published in 1987, on *Broken Arrow*, and over subsequent years, he continued to supply various anecdotes behind the scenes.[2] His two daughters filled in the gaps of their grandfather's busy career with numerous photos and journals. At a black-tie event in New York City, Delmer's widow, former actress Mary Lou Lender, spoke about how she managed to juggle her family life with service in civic affairs while her busy husband wrote, directed, and produced movies all over the world.

One of Delmer's movies took a major step in the breakdown of conventional stereotypes. *Broken Arrow* demonstrates the postwar ideal that Natives and whites can coexist peacefully, each benefiting from the other. The story's Cochise/Jeffords relationship attempted to serve as a model for tolerance between both races while emphasizing that whites must reexamine their prejudices and learn something about Native American culture. Both whites and Apaches do indeed accomplish noble deeds and commit crimes, but in end, the Apache—and not the white—emerges as a hero.

Daves's first Western certainly has its flaws. The Native American people speak English rather than Apache, whites are cast in leading Apache roles, and Apache culture is highly romanticized.[3] Moreover, the film's portrayal of the girl's Puberty Rite or Coming-Of-Age Ceremony is based on Western Apache rather than Chiricahua traditions. Additionally, many scholars agree that the movie lacks the polish of the director's later Western *3:10 to Yuma* (1957), with its evocative cinematography and psychological undertones. But *Broken Arrow* also belongs among his distinctions, for it not only probed the frontier's Indian/white attitudes but established a bond between Native and white people.

Despite its many artistic liberties, *Broken Arrow* contains powerful political and social statements about Hollywood and its attitudes toward Indian/white relations. The film was released after World War II at a time when the industry devoted more serious attention to the race question, particularly in films dealing with Black Americans like *Pinky*, *Home of the Brave*, and *Lost Boundaries* (all 1949). Similarly, Westerns explored racial and ethnic tensions and suggested that American society stand alongside its Native peoples. Daves himself had said that *Broken Arrow* and other pro-Indian Westerns "offered a safe vehicle for unacceptably liberal ideals on racial and political coexistence."[4] (African American newspapers agreed and praised the movie for exposing the Black/white race issue vis-à-vis American Indians.) Many of the film's successors, namely *The Battle at Apache Pass* (1952), *Sitting Bull* (1954), *Taza, Son of Cochise* (1954), and *Walk the Proud Land* (1956), advocated mutual coexistence as a long-term solution for racial relations. Television reiterated the same theme with ABC's spinoff *Broken Arrow* (1956–1958) along with *Brave Eagle* (1955–1957), *Law of the Plainsmen* (1959–1960), and other series.

Broken Arrow was hardly the first film to treat Indians sympathetically. Hollywood had been producing feature films with "friendly" Native images since the 1920s, most notably with *Braveheart* (1925), *The Vanishing American* (1925), *Eskimo* (1933), and *Massacre* (1934). A story similar to *Broken Arrow*'s appeared in the 1932 Western *End of the Trail*, a Columbia movie that shows Captain Tim Travers (Tim McCoy) fighting to protect his Arapaho friends from an unscrupulous Army officer. Like the historical character Thomas Jeffords, Travers persuades the Army to draw up a peace agreement preserving Native lands and becomes an Indian agent. *End of the Trail* was a low-budget B Western, and as only a companion to the main attraction, it eventually faded into obscurity. A later Western, *Fort Apache* (1948), portrays Cochise as a sympathetic character who is "an impressive and dignified man" willing to negotiate.[5] This John Ford movie parallels the US Army's defeat in the Battle of the Little Bighorn with the Apache conflict: Cochise and his warriors lead the cavalry into a trap and emerge as victorious. Unlike *Broken Arrow*, however, *Fort Apache* offers no formal Indian/white peace agreement.

Almost seventy-five years after *Broken Arrow*'s release, its frontier setting and Native American portrayals continue to invite multiple interpretations. Recent scholarship, in fact, has recognized *Broken Arrow* as the first major civil rights–oriented American Indian film produced by Hollywood.[6] Other studies show how prevailing attitudes and expectations toward Hollywood and its Native portrayals have changed over time. Several scholars, for example, have read *Broken Arrow* as a parable of Hollywood communism. At its annual awards dinner in 1992, the Writers Guild of America posthumously awarded the movie's blacklisted screenwriter, Albert Maltz, and restored proper screenwriting credit to him.[7]

Maltz, along with the other Hollywood Ten, had been sent to prison for refusing to cooperate with the House Un-American Activities Committee (HUAC) in its investigation of communist influence in

Hollywood.[8] The film had initially credited Michael Blankfort, who had served as a front for Maltz.

Several scholars thus proposed that Maltz injected much of his own paranoia over communist accusations and crafted *Broken Arrow* as a resistance to McCarthyism.[9] For them, the film's narrative meaning reaches beyond the literal level of Native/white relations and includes parallels between the Cold War and communism.

Author Glenn Frankel offered a similar reading of *High Noon* (1952). Frankel revealed that screenwriter Carl Foreman, who was summoned to appear before HUAC in 1951, much later admitted to crafting the movie as an allegory to the Hollywood blacklist. Foreman readily identified with Marshal Will Kane (Gary Cooper), who stood up against the story's gunmen (members of HUAC) and the town's cowardly citizens (who remained passive or betrayed him like the Hollywood community.) As Foreman explained, "I became that guy. I became the Gary Cooper character."[10] But Maltz never discussed his political beliefs in relation to *Broken Arrow*, nor did he acknowledge any association with the story's main character, Thomas Jeffords.

Still other critics have explored *Broken Arrow*'s theme by treating its Indian characters not allegorically but historically. While I agree that films—especially recent ones—bear some responsibility to respect historical events, movies as an art form reflect the attitudes and themes of an era only by recreating those events and not by documenting the events exactly as they happened.[11] For me, then, *Broken Arrow* emerges as an example of how its creators reshaped history to respond to America's evolving attitudes toward Native Americans.

Additionally, a few scholars proposed that *Broken Arrow* reveals a part of Daves's common theme of a partnership between two heroes. Thus, the

Figure 0.1. Eastern view of Dragoon Mountains in southeastern Arizona. Author's collection.

film's heroes, in this case an Apache and a white, become a central dynamic between two protagonists of seemingly incompatible backgrounds and points of views.[12] Similar relationships appeared in Daves's *Demetrius and the Gladiators* with its former African king and (white) Christian slave; in *3:10 to Yuma* with a ruthless outlaw and a local rancher; and with *Cowboy*'s idealistic tenderfoot and gruff trail boss. In that sense, *Broken Arrow* isn't revealing contemporary social trends as much as it is Daves's own perspective of human relationships.

Broken Arrow was indeed Daves's idealized version of Indian/white relations as personified by its two leading characters. My book will trace how this relationship began with Elliott Arnold's novel *Blood Brother* (1947) then developed into Maltz's screenplay to eventually become a harbinger of postwar liberal Westerns. I will discuss the movie's director and its production at Twentieth Century-Fox along with how *Broken Arrow*'s message of Indian/white tolerance coincided with the government's effort to control Native peoples by "assimilating" (or colonizing) them into American society. Daves indeed had advocated the postwar concept of an Indian/white "brotherhood," but for better or worse, his efforts to transform his Native characters into model white citizens would shape Hollywood Westerns for many years.

1 | The Screenwriter and His Front

Albert Maltz's acclaimed stories of human struggles and his stand against racism were especially timely in a postwar society. But his ongoing membership in the Communist Party drew much suspicion, and before long, he was one of many artists blacklisted by Hollywood. In spite of his political beliefs, the Brooklyn-born screenwriter penned several patriotic World War II–themed movies, and his script for the award-winning short film *The House I Live In* (1945) featured Frank Sinatra preaching tolerance and understanding to a gang of boys who persecute a neighborhood kid for his Jewish heritage. When producer Julian Blaustein asked Maltz to read Elliott Arnold's best-selling novel *Blood Brother* (1947), Maltz valued the opportunity to write a screenplay about his longest-standing human concern—his opposition to racism.[1] Both he and Arnold shared the belief that individuals were able to overcome bigotry within their community. Given the possible political fallout of hiring a blacklisted writer, Maltz needed someone to front for his adaptation of Arnold's novel.

Broken Arrow's journey to the screen thus involved stealth and secrecy.

Figure 1.1. Albert Maltz, blacklisted screenwriter of *Broken Arrow*, 1950s. Courtesy of Marc Wanamaker / Bison Archives.

Maltz was determined to get his message through, that despite inherent differences, Indians and whites can coexist peacefully. Thus, the movie's portrayal of the friendship between two men of completely different backgrounds—an Apache chief and a former mail scout—would set the story's tone. The movie's postwar theme of a universal brotherhood sprang from Arnold's novel and showed that "men need to seek to understand each other," an irony not lost on Maltz and his blacklisted colleagues.[2] Regardless, everyone agreed that the friendship between Thomas Jeffords and Cochise would remain the story's central focus.

The first challenge was that *Blood Brother*'s more than five hundred pages had to be condensed to ninety-three minutes of screen time. According to Arnold, the movie had to omit about 90 percent of the novel.[3] Jeffords himself did not emerge until about one third into the story, long after Arnold's lengthy descriptions of Anglo-Apache relations, Mexican/American conflicts, military battles, and Apache ceremonies.[4]

Arnold traces the growth of Tucson from a small settlement to a prosperous mining town and emphasizes the complex history and harsh life in the Arizona Territory. The author also elaborates on Apache traditions like the trickster tales of coyote and the Puberty Rite or Coming-of-Age Ceremony that celebrate a young girl's transition to adulthood.

Blood Brother covers nineteen years of Southwest history, from 1855, shortly after whites acquired the land south of the Gila River in what is now Arizona, to 1874, the year Cochise died.[5] Initially, the Chiricahua Apache chief Cochise and his band of the Chokonen chose peace between whites and Apaches and broke with Mangas Coloradas, chief of the Mimbreño Apaches, who attempted to drive Mexicans and Americans from ancestral lands. Cochise was able to maintain his agreement honorably until the Army unjustly executed his relatives for a crime they did not commit.[6] The novel is divided into five parts or books: "Cochise," "Jeffords," "Tucson," "Blood Brothers," and "The Final Time."[7] Arnold includes a prelude to the story; the book's main events, he states, are entirely true.[8] The author notes, however, that Jeffords's Apache wife, Sonseeahray, and the character of Terry Weaver (the American girl who later cares for him) are both invented.[9]

The novel's second book picks up with the story of Thomas Jeffords, whose life was animated by wanderlust, drifting from place to place and job to job. Jeffords was born in 1832 in western New York and tried his various skills as a ship's captain (on the Great Lakes), gold miner, prospector, surveyor, and mail courier. In the late 1860s, he was a superintendent of mails between Tucson and Socorro, New Mexico Territory, and paid his riders well. But the increasing conflicts between whites and Apaches prompted him to approach Cochise on friendly terms to offer a peace agreement.[10] Jeffords was a genial fellow who kept to himself and enjoyed an occasional drink or two. He was tall and lanky with a bushy red beard and blue eyes and about thirty-five years old, nearly twenty years younger than the Apache chief. Cochise, on the other hand, was close to six feet tall and well proportioned, with large dark eyes and "a sharp nose that was curved and proud as the beak of an eagle."[11] His long, straight, black hair contained a few silver threads, and his face was painted with red and black streaks. His native language was Chiricahua Apache, but he spoke and understood Spanish as well.[12]

Despite years of hostility between the Chiricahua and white settlers, Jeffords became Cochise's friend and won the trust of his tribe. The crux of Arnold's story occurs when the two men from seemingly incompatible backgrounds symbolically reconcile their differences through a special (and fictitious) "blood brother" ceremony. Jeffords then leads the Civil War hero General Oliver Otis Howard to Cochise's camp to persuade the Chiricahua to settle on a reservation. Howard, who had lost his arm combating Confederate forces during the Civil War, was known as the "Christian general" because his diplomacy was deeply rooted in his evangelical faith. He was commissioner of the Freedman's Bureau from 1865 to 1874 and was both founder and president of Howard University, the historically Black college named after him. Howard was a strong advocate of President Grant's Peace Policy and believed it would encourage Indians to become members of American society. The novel continues with the death of Cochise in 1874.

Arnold was fascinated with Jeffords. "I know of no greater display of courage in the history of the world than this man riding alone into the camp of Cochise," he said.[13] Arnold's roots were far from Apache country. He was born in 1912 in Brooklyn, New York, coincidentally the same year Arizona became a state. At the young age of fifteen, he plunged into the

Figure 1.2. Elliott Arnold, author of *Blood Brother*. Courtesy of the University of Arizona Libraries Special Collections.

newspaper business and later attended New York University. His career as a feature writer took off at the *New York World-Telegram*, but by then, he had already written his first of twenty-five novels and other books. Arnold joined the Army Air Corps in 1942 and fought in the Mediterranean and Pacific, where he rose to captain and received a Bronze Star.[14] His military experience would serve as an inspiration for his later novels, including the 1967 best-seller about the Danish Underground, *A Night of Watching*, which shared with *Blood Brother* a similar theme of heroes fighting a widespread social prejudice.[15]

Arnold credited his Arizonan wife for the idea behind *Blood Brother*. Unlike her husband, who had an Eastern background, Helen Emmons had roots in the Far West. In 1876, her mother's parents settled as pioneers in Cochise County, where most of the story of *Blood Brother* occurs and where she was born in 1919. Arnold met Emmons when he was stationed at Tucson's Davis-Monthan Army Air Field, and the couple married in

1943.[16] When she told her husband about a Cochise/Jeffords story she had read in an *Arizona Highways* magazine, Arnold was hooked.[17] He believed that the peace agreement between two completely different men struck a universal note and became a parable of "how sworn enemies, with understanding, can find a common ground for peace" within a troubled postwar world.[18] The author would soon venture into the mountains of southeastern Arizona and convince his wife to leave their Maine home and settle in Tucson, nearly three thousand miles away.[19]

Blood Brother's publication was timely. Two years after the book appeared, Twentieth Century-Fox purchased the novel's worldwide motion picture rights. The idea for *Broken Arrow* originated when Julian Blaustein left his position as editorial supervisor for David O. Selznick and became an independent producer. Blaustein believed that *Blood Brother* was "a Western with a point of view" and that its pitch for "the treatment of minorities, in this case some Indians" was long overdue.[20] He initially hoped to produce the film independently but ultimately turned to Fox, where studio head Darryl F. Zanuck, vice president of production, liked the script and purchased it.[21]

Zanuck took a hands-on approach and oversaw every detail of movie making for his studio, including changes to plot and characterization. As Fox screenwriter and producer Nunnally Johnson explained, "There was none of this the-director-takes-charge while Zanuck was making a picture. The director never took charge. Zanuck was in charge."[22] Still, Zanuck's films were noteworthy for confronting issues of race and prejudice in American society. He had exposed anti-Semitism as early as 1934 in *The House of Rothschild* and later with *Gentleman's Agreement* (1947). *Susannah of the Mounties* (1939) preached racial harmony vis-à-vis a young Canadian Blackfoot boy and a preadolescent Shirley Temple, and *Pinky*

Figure 1.3. Darryl F. Zanuck, vice president of production at Twentieth Century-Fox, 1949. Courtesy of Marc Wanamaker / Bison Archives.

(1949) explored Southern bigotry though a mixed-race woman (passing for white) and her love for a white doctor. *No Way Out* (1950) featured Sidney Poitier in a debut performance as a Black doctor who confronts racism when a young white criminal is shot by police and dies under his care. The man's brother, a raging sociopath (Richard Widmark), accuses the physician of murder and initiates a campaign of vengeance. Despite the movie's explosive subject matter, Zanuck was determined to tell the story from a Black perspective. "We are going to show the kind of hate the Negro runs up against in his daily life, how he is afraid to walk on certain streets," he said.[23] *Broken Arrow* would likewise challenge white attitudes toward America's Native peoples.

Blaustein and Arnold quickly hit it off. Both apparently saw eye to eye on how to transfer the novel to the screen and agreed completely about the spirit of the picture.[24] The producer's choice to adapt the novel was the blacklisted screenwriter Albert Maltz, whose previous stories of human struggles and his stand against racism coincided with Arnold's ideals. "I felt that I had attached myself to a movement that was going to bring about human brotherhood and an end to all discrimination in the world," Maltz said of his beliefs that apparently dovetailed with the author's theme.[25] The screenwriter had already added several patriotic World War II–themed movies to his credits including Fritz Lang's *Cloak and Dagger* (1946) along with Delmer Daves's *Destination Tokyo* (1943) and *Pride of the Marines* (1945).

But *Blood Brother*'s journey to the screen included political accusations and sworn secrecy. Maltz valued the opportunity to write a screenplay on his opposition to racism, but his ongoing membership in the Communist Party remained problematic. In October 1947, HUAC launched its investigation into allegations of communist influence in the motion picture industry, and Maltz emerged as one of the prominent screenwriters and directors known as the Hollywood Ten. When the Ten appeared before the committee, they stonewalled and refused to answer any questions. Maltz reminded the committee of his patriotic movies and his novel *The Cross and the Arrow* (1944), a story about moral resistance within Nazi Germany that was distributed in a special armed services edition to military members abroad.[26] His testimony was to no avail. The refusal of Maltz and other members of the Hollywood Ten to cooperate with the committee prompted Congress to cite them for contempt. In 1950, after a long series of trials and appeals, Maltz was sentenced to a year in prison and a fine of $1,000.[27]

Regardless of Maltz's political troubles, Blaustein believed he had good reason to hire the screenwriter. Maltz was distinguished for his modern screenplays, including the gritty melodrama *This Gun for Hire* (1942) and *The Naked City* (1948), but his stories were also known for their "high spiritual and humanistic qualities," their concern for people, and an idealism seldom seen on the screen.[28] Those qualities easily coincided with Arnold's ability to flesh out his characters' sensibilities. But Maltz's problems only grew worse when Fox abruptly canceled its plans to film his short novel *The Journey of Simon McKeever*, a tale of a "spunky septuagenarian" and his hitchhiking search for an arthritis cure.[29] The studio gave no apparent reason for its about-face, although anti-communist church groups reportedly had threatened Fox with boycotts and picketing.[30] Meanwhile, Maltz had joined the other nine blacklisted artists fighting the committee's conviction, which the Supreme Court eventually refused to consider.[31]

With the dark cloud of HUAC hovering over him, Maltz realized he needed a writer to front for his adaptation of Arnold's novel. Michael Blankfort, a former prison psychologist and Broadway writer, director, and producer, agreed to lend his name and provide revisions.[32] Blankfort had drawn on his clinical skills for his screenplay of *Blind Alley* (1939) and its 1948 remake *The Dark Past*, both Columbia low-budget thrillers of a kind of cat-and-mouse game between a ruthless killer and his psychologist hostage. He had known Maltz from his days at the Theatre Union, a group in New York City whose dramas about social problems attracted large working-class audiences. Blankfort, aware that his friend had a wife and family to support, secretly signed a contract and engaged Maltz to do the major portion of the work, offering him 90 percent of the $15,000 writer's fee. Blaustein, meanwhile, was privy to the arrangement and secretly ran Blankfort's changes by Maltz. Not even Maltz's agent or anyone in the studio—save for Blaustein—knew of the clandestine arrangement.[33] "If this [arrangement] had gotten out," said author and HUAC historian Larry Ceplair, "it would have killed the careers of both Blankfort and Blaustein."[34]

Amid all this behind-the-scenes subterfuge, everyone—from Arnold,

Figure 1.4. Michael Blankfort, "front" for Albert Maltz. Courtesy of Marc Wanamaker / Bison Archives.

Blankfort, and Blaustein to Maltz and Zanuck—agreed that peace and racial tolerance would be central to the picture's theme. Various theories have proposed that Maltz adapted *Blood Brother* as a resistance to accusations of communism in Hollywood. But unlike Carl Foreman's recollections of the postwar communist influence on *High Noon,* Maltz never discussed *Broken Arrow* as a parable of Cold War tension nor as an allegory to the Hollywood blacklist. In fact, years earlier, Maltz had criticized his fellow communists for placing politics above art in an article for the Marxist magazine *The New Masses.* "I have come to believe that the accepted understanding of art as a weapon is not a useful guide, but a straitjacket," he wrote in 1945, although party members forced him to recant two months later.[35]

Maltz had no intention to frame his *Blood Brother* screenplay as a message film beyond what he and Blaustein agreed to. "I never considered that

I was going to try and use films to express my political attitudes," Maltz attempted to explain years later. "Certainly they *reflected* attitudes that I had and these were manifested in the way that my characters spoke and what they thought about and so forth."[36] In the foreword to his script, Maltz described *Blood Brother* only as a historical narrative that should "convey the quality of authenticity present in a documentary." To that end, his few notes advised that the movie be photographed in the location where the events actually occurred and that Apaches be used in the cast.[37]

Maltz chose to focus on the Cochise/Jeffords's relationship and omit the novel's lengthy background of Chiricahua history and culture. The novel *Blood Brother* opens with an omniscient narrator's point of view and provides background into Cochise and his legacy, describing an Apache victory celebration following the successful raid of a Mexican village. Arnold elaborates on details such as the warriors' regalia and face paint, the music of the women, and the slaughter of animals for the feast. He concludes with a meeting of the Chiricahua in which Cochise proposes to make peace with the Americans. Those warriors who disagree leave the Chiricahua, electing Geronimo as their leader, a version of which appears in the film toward the end.

Maltz's screenplay reduces the novel's lengthy time span to two years.[38] He shifts the focus from Cochise and instead opens with a flashback told from Jeffords's point of view. His script highlights the friendship between Jeffords (James Stewart) and Cochise (Jeff Chandler), with historical information secondary to the two men's relationship. The writer's 1948 initial draft (also titled *Blood Brother*) is similar to the final film, which begins with Jeffords's narration of the events describing how he aided Machogee, a wounded Apache boy. The Chiricahua capture Jeffords but eventually turn him loose with a warning to stay out of Apache country.

The Apache continue to kill government mail riders, and Jeffords resolves to make peace with their chief. He enlists Juan, an Apache aide, to teach him their language and lead him to Cochise. But hatred against the Apache runs deep, and Tucson's citizens, including Jeffords's young female friend Terry, are dubious of his efforts.[39]

The lynching scene in the movie was absent from Maltz's script.[40] Studio head Zanuck had already grappled with mob violence and a lynching in the disturbing 1943 Western *The Ox-Bow Incident,* which featured a Black preacher who sympathized with the white victims. During a conference, Zanuck himself suggested adding a lynching scene to *Broken Arrow* in which the angry townsfolk would attempt to hang Jeffords until General Howard intervenes.[41] The scene prompted a few scholars to interpret the Jeffords character as a metaphor for the screen's blacklisted writer facing the community's rejection and to argue that the townspeople emerge as barely disguised communist witch-hunters who target Jeffords as a traitor for befriending the Apache.[42] Arguably, Zanuck's addition served to heighten the story's tension by creating a sharp divide between the town's racist citizens and Jeffords's pro-Indian sympathies.

Angry townsfolk notwithstanding, *Broken Arrow* minimizes most of the tensions leading to the present conflicts. The immediate concern is for the government mail riders who must travel through Apache country yet seldom return alive. The novel instead traces the growth of anti-Indian attitudes in the Southwest over many years by revealing how white immigration resulted in further encroachment on Apache territory and more atrocities on both sides. Arnold recounts in detail the tragic meeting in 1861 between Cochise and the youthful (and inexperienced) Lieutenant George Bascom, a West Point graduate whose misdirected zeal ignites a decade-long war between the Chiricahua and whites. For years, Cochise had been at peace with Americans and thought that Bascom's invitation was another attempt at conciliation. But Bascom lures the Apache chief into a trap and falsely accuses him of kidnapping a twelve-year-old boy.[43] The Army unjustly hangs Cochise's relatives and inadvertently launches a war in which no settler—or his livestock—was safe. Jeffords only alludes to these events at a dinner scene in *Broken Arrow*, thereby reducing nearly a decade of events to minimal dialogue.[44]

Broken Arrow minimizes the roles of several other characters as it shifts the focus to the Cochise/Jeffords relationship. In *Blood Brother*, Cochise has two wives (and later a third), but in the movie, only one, Nalikadeya, appears, and members of his family—his brothers (Coyuntura and Juan), two sons (Taza and Naiche), and two daughters (Dash-den-zhoos, and Naithlotonz)—are not seen. The film's elimination of Cochise's family thus reduces the tribal nature of Apache culture and spotlights the Cochise/Jeffords relationship as primary.

Significant non–Native American characters are also absent in the film. General Howard's trusty aide-de-camp, Lieutenant Joseph A. Sladen, who accompanied him on his visit to Cochise, disappears in the movie version.[45] Jeffords's female friend Terry is hardly noticeable; she briefly shows up in a scene at the dinner table swatting flies, but he barely acknowledges her presence. Terry is a recurring character in the novel and pressures Jeffords for years to begin a romantic relationship. Her presence (and constant nagging) detracts from the overall story and Jeffords's relations with the Apache. Zanuck had suggested adding a scene that would reveal a romantic relationship between Jeffords and Terry, but the film eliminates Terry as a rival to Sonseeahray to instead focus on Apache/white relations.[46]

The character of General Howard (Basil Ruysdael) remains key to the story's peace agreement. His Christian ideals support the movie's message that a harmonious relationship between Apaches and whites—rather than bloody wars—will bring peace to the region. The tall, white-bearded religious crusader has a soft and gentle manner. Nevertheless, Jeffords is at first skeptical of Howard's missionary zeal until the general explains that his Bible "preaches brotherhood for all of God's children." Jeffords, still dubious, questions whether God's children have to be white. "My Bible says nothing about the pigmentation of the skin," Howard replies, the movie's reminder that America's postwar society embraces all races.[47]

Additionally, the movie more closely follows Geronimo's transformation from a loyal warrior to a renegade. Geronimo (Jay Silverheels), a warrior and medicine man from the Bedonkohe band of Chiricahua, breaks from Cochise in *Blood Brother*'s first book and returns shortly after to face a severe tongue-lashing by his chief. He then fades into the background.[48] But Maltz gives Geronimo a more substantial role and moves his departure to much later in the story. In *Broken Arrow*, Geronimo first appears in the opening sequence when he and the Chiricahua capture and kill several white miners. He is one of two warriors flanking Cochise when Jeffords enters the Apache camp, and he sits beside Jeffords during the Crown Dance. The loyal Apache warrior fights alongside Cochise during a military ambush and boasts of destroying wagons and seizing supplies. But he ultimately defies the peace agreement between General Howard and Cochise by announcing, "I walk away."[49] Only then does Cochise banish him from the tribe. Geronimo's brusque departure in *Broken Arrow* would establish an essential theme in 1950s Westerns that "good" Indians accept white peace terms but "bad" (i.e., renegade) Indians do not (see chapter 4).

Blood Brother was a part of the trend toward greater realism in the American Western that resulted in Apaches becoming more recognizable as human beings. The novel's portrayal of Cochise thus exposes his strengths as well as deep flaws. Once known as a fierce enemy of whites, he emerges as a complex character rather than a noble or fiendish stereotype.[50] Arnold's description of the Apache leader testifies to a certain poise and dignity with a kind of aura; he was "a very tall man and on his horse, larger than any other, his stature was almost heroic."[51] Cochise was both a formidable warrior and an astute negotiator of peace; he held remarkable power over his tribe and could outmaneuver the military's most skillful leaders. Both Apaches and whites respected his word and knew that he honored "two things more than anything else in men: truth and bravery."[52] So determined was the Apache chief to never break his word that when the US government delayed essential supplies to the reservation and the Chiricahua nearly starved during the cold winter months, Cochise still upheld his side of the agreement.

But the author also depicts a leader who suffers from his own human weaknesses. Cochise, enraged at the betrayal of the US Army for the Bascom affair, vowed to avenge his family's murder and surrendered himself to violence for more than ten years. Arnold himself describes Cochise as falling into despair and turning into "a living legend of death and horror."[53] The Apache chief summoned his father-in-law, Mangas Coloradas, and the Mimbreño to a war of extermination against all Americans and swore to kill ten white-eyes for every Indian slain.[54] His deep-rooted animosity toward Mexicans (they had murdered his father and supplied their government with Apache scalps) drove him to capture his enemies and resort to some of the most gruesome tortures known to his ancestors. Cochise attempted to drown his anger with *tiswin* (an alcoholic beverage brewed from corn) and physically lashed out at his wives. He had a quick temper and maintained a zero-tolerance policy toward his own warriors by summarily executing those who transgressed.[55]

Yet behind the warrior's tough armor existed a hint of vulnerability. The fierce Apache chief, noted for his brutality, liked to carry around his favorite red blanket. Arnold explains how a prominent Arizona cattle rancher had gifted the fine woolen item to the Chiricahua chief and wove his name into it. Cochise would proudly wrap himself in the blanket and was even buried in it.[56]

The movie *Broken Arrow* strips Cochise of his flaws (and his red blanket) and replaces them with an aura of honor and valor. Maltz describes him as "greater than other men" who "is bigger in stature than most of the other Apaches."[57] In contrast to the novel's Apache chief, the movie portrays Cochise as a "victimized saint" who arguably represents more of white culture's imagination than a complex human being.[58] He is also the story's noble or romantic savage, with near-perfect English that is especially apparent when compared to Stewart's simple, drawling speech. The difference was not lost on one reviewer who complained that Cochise carries himself like a decathlon champion at the Olympic Games and speaks with the "phrasing of a salutatorian of a graduating class."[59]

Broken Arrow establishes Cochise's noble stature during his first meeting with Jeffords. The frontiersman enters the Chiricahua camp, dismounts his horse, then calmly hands his weapons to an elderly Apache and says, "Hold these things for me. I will need them when I leave." Jeffords then praises Cochise as a great leader who respects truth and bravery. The camera frames Cochise against the vast horizon, flanked by two warriors and gazing at Jeffords down below. The Apache chief then asserts his authority by undermining Jeffords's presence. "How do you know you will leave here alive?" he asks. "I am Cochise. Speak."[60]

Despite the tense encounter, *Broken Arrow* sets a tone of racial tolerance and equality early. Cochise invites Jeffords into a wikiup then

Figure 1.5. Cochise (Jeff Chandler) speaks with Jeffords (James Stewart) in Broken Arrow. Author's collection.

motions for him to sit down first. The low camera angle looking upward further asserts the dominance of the Apache chief; he towers over Jeffords and stares down at him. During their initial meeting, Jeffords tries to convince Cochise to allow the mail riders to travel unharmed through the Arizona Territory. Cochise tells him, "You're a brave man," then sits opposite him.[61] The two now face each other in the same frame while Jeffords lays the foundation for a friendship and proposes that he and Cochise live together as brothers. "Walk with me so my people will see us together," the Chiricahua chief says, a reminder that neither man regards race nor color as barriers to their relationship.[62]

Broken Arrow further reinforces Cochise's heroic stature when he summarily eliminates a fellow warrior who disobeys. In the novel *Blood*

Brother, Nahilzay, one of Cochise's warriors, unexpectedly attacks Jeffords while sleeping. Cochise had promised that Jeffords would be safe and protected among the Apache and accuses Nahilzay of betrayal. Jeffords insists that he enact his own vengeance for the transgression and challenges Nahilzay to a duel with knives, mortally wounding the Apache warrior. But in *Broken Arrow,* Cochise prevails, and he, rather than Jeffords, promptly kills Nahilzay (John War Eagle).[63] Like the Geronimo character, Nahilzay is the renegade Indian who rejects white peace terms and is eliminated.

The film also emphasizes that Cochise's battle tactics are superior to the US Army's. Arnold's novel describes how the Chiricahua warriors swoop down on a Mexican village during a raid and outmaneuver its inhabitants by attacking in flanks.[64] But in *Broken Arrow,* the enemy instead becomes a battalion of well-armed Army soldiers. The scene begins when an overly confident colonel leads General Howard and the soldiers through the open valley while Apache warriors peer from high above. Notes on Maltz's script emphasize that the colonel is in charge although he naively dismisses Howard's warning of an ambush.[65] The Chiricahua chief then signals four flanks of his warriors, who one by one attack the Army from multiple directions instead of all pouncing at once. In a cleverly planned attack, the Apache ambush the wagons, steal the supplies, and kill the soldiers who appear faceless and die en masse. The body of the Apache boy Machogee, however, lies peacefully in the foreground as if to personalize his loss.

The confrontation eerily recalls depictions of the Battle of the Little Bighorn, with riderless horses and dead soldiers scattered across the landscape and long lances protruding from the bodies.[66] The colonel is among the casualties, but the one-armed general rises unharmed from the carnage looking somewhat bewildered. He realizes that under Cochise's command, the Chiricahua have proven themselves formidable opponents to the US Army.[67]

While *Broken Arrow* depicts Cochise as a noble leader with no apparent flaws, Jeffords's virtuous character troubled Zanuck. In Maltz's script, Jeffords appoints himself messenger to the Chiricahua and eagerly plunges into dangerous Apache territory because he believes he is "the one white man with enough sense to do something."[68] But Zanuck objected to the character's self-righteous behavior and complained that nobility simply oozes out of Jeffords who is never wrong about anything. The audience must know what makes Jeffords willing to risk his life to bring about peace, Zanuck reasoned, or at least to see something that goads him into doing it. "[Jeffords] is so completely noble and untarnished, so uncompromisingly lofty in his ideals," Zanuck said, "that I found myself asking: 'What makes this man tick? What motivated him to go to Cochise in the first place?'"[69]

At the very least, Jeffords needed to be an adversary to the intimidating but intelligent Cochise. The movie thus shows that Jeffords is at first reluctant to prove himself a hero before considering any risky venture. Further modifications in the opening narration expose the character's deep prejudice when he sees the wounded boy: "His kind was more dangerous than a snake. He was an Apache."[70]

Arnold's fictitious "blood-brother" ceremony seals the friendship between Cochise and Jeffords. The author actually repeats the ritual three times, beginning when Cochise exchanges blood with Mangas Coloradas followed by the marriage ceremony between Jeffords and Sonseeahray.[71] Later, shortly before Cochise and Jeffords meet Howard, a more elaborate ritual occurs. The two men kneel facing each other, and the medicine man cuts open the flesh in each man's arm and collects the flowing blood into two separate silver goblets. He ties together both arms so that the incisions cover each, allowing their blood to commingle, and then orders both men to drink. Cochise says, "We are no longer friends. . . . We now are brothers."[72]

The novel's mingling and drinking of the blood with its quasi-religious overtones have puzzled many readers. Jeffords reportedly said nothing about such a ritual, but when he died in 1914, several Tucson newspapers claimed that "the two were 'blood-brothers,' made so by the mystical ceremony of the intermingling and supping of blood from each other's arms."[73] But authorities of Apache culture deny that any blood-brother ritual exists in Chiricahua tradition, and both Maltz's script and Daves's movie omit the farcical ceremony.[74]

Broken Arrow's wedding instead becomes the novel's blood-brother ritual displaced into marriage. The movie resembles the author's passages regarding the wedding, although no such ceremony exists in Apache culture.[75] Regardless, the mingling of blood between a white man and a Native woman illustrates the film's symbolic union of two races and cultures within the broader context of American society. As Jeffords and Sonseeahray (Debra Paget) kneel, the medicine man makes a small incision of Jeffords's right hand and Sonseeahray's left hand and ties both hands together. Their blood mingles and the medicine man recites: "There are two bodies but now there is but one blood in both of them."[76] Following the wedding, the bride and groom ride white horses to a secret hiding place, presumably to consummate their marriage.[77]

The marriage, however, does not survive. In the novel, Sonseeahray is pregnant with her first child and dies from a soldier's bullet during a raid. Jeffords drifts aimlessly for months and eventually becomes an Apache scout. But Sonseeahray's death fails to create any profound change

Figure 1.6. *Broken Arrow*'s Apache wedding ceremony with Debra Paget, James Stewart, and Chris Willow Bird as the spiritual leader. Author's collection.

between Apache and white societies. Cochise and General Howard later reach an agreement that the US government set aside the Chiricahua Indian Reservation in southeastern Arizona, with Jeffords appointed its special agent. Two years after Cochise's death, Jeffords became disillusioned with the government's reservation policies and resigned his post as Chiricahua agent.[78] Forty years later, Jeffords died quite suddenly and quietly as he "lay down and closed his eyes and embarked on the final journey to discover at last whether he would meet his old friend 'up there, beyond that hill.'"[79] The reservation may have been a dismal failure, but the author's main point is that the friendship between Cochise and Jeffords survived the surrounding bigotry and corruption.

Twentieth Century-Fox, however, wanted a more universal and profound message. Maltz himself had incorporated Arnold's ending, which emphasized the main theme of the story—the friendship of two men of different cultures.[80] Initially, the script called for Jeffords to narrate the conclusion, referring to Cochise's death and burial: "And I said a proud farewell to a great man, who had lived and died with truth and honor."[81] In the final script, however, Cochise does not die, and he delivers a speech forbidding Jeffords to avenge Sonseeahray's murder. The theme of an Apache/white peaceful coexistence dominates the conclusion: Cochise narrates that Jeffords brought peace to the land and would always have a home with his people.[82]

Broken Arrow thus highlights the peace agreement at the expense of the reservation's demise. The movie's conclusion was modified to show that Sonseeahray's death brings peace between Apaches and whites, but Cochise—and not Jeffords—emerges as the story's hero. Jeffords, in fact, threatens to break the fragile peace agreement that he and Cochise worked so hard for. The frontiersman is nearly hysterical and demands vengeance when a group of Indian-hating settlers lure the Apache into a trap and kill his wife.[83] But Cochise instead scolds him: "Are you a child that you thought peace would come easy? You, who taught me so well? Is it my brother who asks me to spit on my word?" The Apache chief reminds Jeffords that he will not betray his people, adding, "And no one on my territory will open war again. Not even you."[84]

Notably, Sonseeahray's death occurs after the peace agreement and thus becomes integral to the film's final moments. Her murder elicits grief from all parties then tests Jeffords's commitment to peace. Thus, a familiar cinematic event takes on its own meaning: Sonseeahray is not a "transgressor" but instead a martyr in the cause for peace and racial harmony.[85]

Figure 1.7. Sonseeahray's death in *Broken Arrow*, with James Stewart holding Debra Paget. Author's collection.

(As discussed in chapter 2, Daves recycled the same theme with the death of Toby in *Drum Beat*.)

Thus, *Broken Arrow*'s community of Apache and settlers joins Jeffords and Cochise to reinforce their commitment to peace. General Howard embraces the opportunity to call off the war and reminds Jeffords that "your very loss has brought our people together in the will to peace. Without that will, treaties are worth little or nothing."[86] (Historically, the US government created the Chiricahua Indian Reservation not by treaty but by Executive Order.[87]) Cochise does not die, and *Broken Arrow*'s optimistic conclusion reverts to Jeffords's narration as he rides alone in the wilderness. His closing words reinforce the peace agreement as well as the movie's message of a postwar brotherhood between Apaches and whites: "But as time passed I came to know that the death of Sonseeahray put a seal on the peace."[88]

The Hollywood ending of peace and brotherly love would not extend to its two writers, however. The film received plenty of kudos; actor Jeff Chandler, screenwriter Michael Blankfort, and cinematographer Ernest Palmer all earned Academy Award nominations. The Writers Guild honored Blankfort—unaware it was mostly the work of Maltz—for the Best Written American Western, and the Golden Globes named *Broken Arrow* the Best Film Promoting International Understanding. But Maltz, locked in a federal prison, could not celebrate or even share his pride with his colleagues. For a short while, he remained fiercely loyal to both Blankfort and Blaustein and knew even the slightest leak about their clandestine arrangement would damage their careers.

In the spring of 1951, Maltz went directly from prison to a self-imposed exile in Mexico, where he lived and wrote under pseudonyms for eleven years.[89] Still, his career suffered. Scripts with Maltz's name were banned in Hollywood, while his books also became forbidden material.[90]

In 1960, Frank Sinatra, who fifteen years earlier had collaborated with Maltz on *The House I Live In*, tried to defy the blacklist by hiring the ostracized screenwriter to adapt *The Execution of Private Slovik*, the true story of the only American soldier executed for desertion during World War II. But public pressure and attacks by the Hearst newspapers and the American Legion eventually forced Sinatra to fire his own writer.[91]

Maltz had already felt the sting of betrayal. In 1951, director Edward Dmytryk, one of the Hollywood Ten who had served time with Maltz at the Mill Point Prison Camp in West Virginia, returned to Washington and denounced his fellow members and named close friends as communists. Maltz was sickened. "The truth about Dmytryk was simple and ugly," he wrote.[92] The following year, his close friend and fellow screenwriter Blankfort testified as a "friendly witness" before HUAC. Unlike Maltz, who openly defied the committee, Blankfort buckled under pressure and criticized the Hollywood Ten. Although Blankfort did not name anyone to the committee, he renounced his political beliefs and naively revealed the names of his ex-wife and cousin when stating that he did not know them to be communists.[93] Maltz, shocked at Blankfort's apparent about-face, accused him of betraying "himself and everything he had once decently stood for" and promptly terminated their long-standing friendship.[94] Many years later, Blankfort tried to extend an olive branch to his former political ally, but Maltz staunchly refused. "If there was anything 'to have out' between us, you would have written me thirteen years ago. Asking for a confrontation now is absurd and masochistic," Maltz snapped. "I have no inner need to play neurotic games with you."[95]

The painful rejection hit Blankfort hard. "The one man who has never forgiven me is Albert Maltz," he lamented years later. "He wouldn't acknowledge the death of my father, whom he knew quite well."[96] For the rest of his life, Blankfort felt indebted to Maltz. "It is growing more and more a burden for me to keep hold of the 'solo' credit which I've borne for these 25 years or so," Blankfort wrote of the *Broken Arrow* screenplay.[97] He contemplated going public with their secret authorship but died unexpectedly in 1982 before anything materialized.[98] Two years later, his widow, Dorothy, wrote of her late husband's sacrifice. "Michael Blankfort put his name on the script as an act of friendship," she said. "He couldn't know at the time that the script would be bought, or that it would be made into a film with his name on it as the sole writer. This was a burden he had to carry down the years. It was his decision finally to make the facts known."[99]

A year after Blankfort's death, Maltz authorized Ceplair to make known his role in *Broken Arrow*.[100] Maltz died on April 26, 1985, and in 1991, the Academy of Motion Picture Arts and Sciences finally awarded him solo credit for the movie and removed Blankfort's name from the nomination. With the restoration of Maltz as screenwriter, his message of a universal brotherhood between people of all backgrounds and races had managed to prevail, at least on the movie screen.

2 | A Director's Vision

Delmer Daves shared a screenwriting background with Maltz and Blankfort and had a passion for America's Natives. Moreover, he wanted *Broken Arrow* to reflect the Apache point of view. "I have a great respect for Indians," he told his alma mater newspaper, *The Stanford Daily*, "and I tried to show this in my film."[1] The filmmaker had directed war movies and gritty melodramas but was especially attracted to *Broken Arrow*'s story of a peaceful coexistence between Apaches and whites. "I tried to make a film that would make you proud of the Indians, that would show the honor the white man *didn't* have," he said of his first Western in which whites as well as Apaches would be both heroes and villains.[2] Ultimately, *Broken Arrow* would reflect Daves's own fascination with Native Americans and his attempt to understand their relationship to white society.

The filmmaker's family heritage had sparked an interest in the subject. Delmer Lawrence Daves was born in San Francisco on July 24, 1904, the second eldest of five children. His father, Arthur Lawrence Daves (1880–1933), married Nana Power Funge (1881–1955) about 1901 and supported the family as a milliner, or hatmaker.[3] Stories of his Irish and Welsh ancestors crossing the country fascinated young Delmer. He grew

Figure 2.1. Delmer Daves, 1961. Courtesy of Marc Wanamaker / Bison Archives.

up hearing about how family members journeyed West in an ox-drawn covered wagon, hauling supplies through Indian country and bouncing across the Sierra Mountain range.[4] A few of his distant relatives had settled in Cochise County as miners, not far from where the historical story of *Broken Arrow* actually took place.[5] "*Broken Arrow* was a dedication to my grandfather and to my father's family," Daves recalled years later. "This is all part and parcel of my heritage."[6]

These family stories later inspired Daves to embark on a rather "insane expedition," or so his parents thought. As a Stanford undergraduate, Daves juggled his studies in law with a variety of campus activities, including acting.[7] He impressed his peers with numerous leading roles in everything from broad comedy to Shakespeare, prompting the school newspaper to note that "his ability as an actor is not to be questioned."[8] Neither was his ability questioned as president of his class of

1926, director of glee club musicals, president of "Sword and Sandals" (the Men's Honorary Dramatic Society), and a member of three campus fraternities.[9] He also found time to design numerous ink sketches for Stanford's yearbook, a talent that would resurface years later when he created storyboards for his movies.

The industrious student said that he even managed to earn $10,000 while attending school and upon graduation headed out to the wilds of northern Arizona. Naturally, his anxious parents questioned his motives. "I think because of grandpa," he told them. "I don't know why, but I want to do it."[10] So for three months, Daves wandered through Navajo and Hopi country while he painted, wrote, and slept under the stars with curious coyotes keeping him company. During that same trip, Daves discovered the red rock cliffs of Sedona, Arizona, and would return nearly twenty-four years later to film *Broken Arrow*.[11]

Daves recalled that his first acting job was an uncredited role in a 1914 film when he was invited to sing in an Episcopal church choir.[12] But his first real credit as an actor occurred when director James Cruze of *The Covered Wagon* (1923) cast him as the heavy Bossy Edwards in *The Duke Steps Out* (1929). Daves liked to boast about how he was able to grab and villainously kiss Joan Crawford while the hero William Haines looked helplessly on.[13] Director Sam Wood then gave the budding actor his first opportunity as a writer for the MGM romantic comedy *So This Is College* (1929).[14]

For the next fourteen years, Daves produced stories and screenplays for approximately twenty-five films, mostly melodramas and musicals. Although Daves was a Republican (he eventually switched to Democrat during the Watergate scandal), critics have linked his work to a "progressive, liberal cinema" in which his scripts revealed a sympathy for different races and a compassion for the class struggles between the working poor and industrial capitalists.[15] Scholars have described Daves as a somewhat modest Hollywood filmmaker who handled assignments competently and professionally but whose films lack the kind of distinct perspective and visual style detected in the works of a John Ford or a Howard Hawks. Daves was never a celebrity director, but he was a talented artist with a distinct worldview in which cooperation between races and ethnic groups was an essential element of American society.[16]

Daves's screenplay for *Stranded*, a 1935 Warner Bros. film, shows noticeable sympathy for working-class struggles. The movie features a hard-boiled construction engineer (George Brent) and a kindhearted social worker (Kay Francis) fighting a union-busting racketeer. Ultimately, a loyal worker exposes the corruption and prevents a strike, and the happy crew celebrate their victory. During *Stranded*, Daves became involved with Francis, at that time one of Warner's leading actresses. Indeed, the glamorous socialite with her cadre of male lovers (including Maurice Chevalier) was quite the opposite of the studious-looking Daves, whom she described as "tall, red-headed, intelligent, not handsome, and very quiet."[17] The affair ended within a few years, and while working as screenwriter for the Harold Lloyd comedy *Professor Beware* (1938), Daves met his future wife, Mary Lou Lender, who had a feature role. She was twenty, and he was thirty-three, and the two married a month after the film's release.[18] Mary Lou (a.k.a. Mary Lawrence) easily kept up with her husband's busy schedule while raising three kids and entertaining the many celebrities who would drop by the house for dinner parties or a dip in the pool. Her recurring TV roles kept her close to home, and later in life, she authored three books on art and was active in local civic groups.[19] Her industrious husband, meanwhile, took up an impressive list of hobbies, including

Figure 2.2. Home of Delmer Daves, 2023. Author's collection.

mineralogy, Gothic lettering, photography, and woodcarving. He was even proficient in Celtic tongues and edited a dictionary in Sanskrit.[20] The marriage lasted thirty-nine years until Daves's death in 1977.

Daves held strong patriotic ideals toward America, as evident in several of his World War II films. Yet he readily acknowledged other cultures—including Native Americans—and viewed the rest of the world with the same respect.[21] His first opportunity to direct came in 1943 when his research on submarine warfare was extensive enough for Warner Bros. to hire him for *Destination Tokyo*, starring Cary Grant and John Garfield. (Daves's son, Michael, and daughter, Deborah, played the children of Grant's character.) Daves also shared screenwriting credit with Albert Maltz, and their story about a US submarine on a secret mission to Japan featured a Greek, an Irishman, and an atheist among its diverse crew.

A year later, Daves wrote and directed *Hollywood Canteen* (1944), an all-star musical revue about a Hollywood entertainment club for service members. The Warner Bros. movie included the all-Black Golden Gate Quartet, whose song "The General Jumped at Dawn" championed multiracial cooperation during the war. The sprightly team enters the stage rolling on a bomb while singing "There were white men, black men on the beam, a real solid all-American team . . . with every creed and color and every belief from an Eskimo to an Indian chief."[22]

Daves easily shifted from one genre to another. Along with his musical and war pictures, he also directed and wrote the Warner Bros. suspense thriller *Dark Passage* (1947), a dreamlike noir story as told through the eyes of a convicted killer featuring Humphrey Bogart and Lauren Bacall. (Both Michael and Deborah again make brief appearances in the movie.) *The Red House* (1947) stars Edward G. Robinson, whose character has buried a terrible secret in the nearby woods. Conversely, *A Kiss in the Dark* (1949) is a romantic comedy about a retired concert pianist (David Niven) who falls in love with an attractive model (Jane Wyman). "To me, what was really remarkable was his range," said his son, Michael, referring to Daves's array of stories. "He could do so many kinds of films and do them well."[23]

Michael Daves (1939–2022), the eldest of his father's three children, worked three summers on the set of his father's Westerns and referred to himself as "an industry brat."[24] Despite his movie roles alongside a few notable stars, he had no desire to become an actor. He eventually became an assistant director on seventeen films and first assistant director on fifty.[25] After retirement, Michael returned to the French colonial–style

Figure 2.3. Private library of Delmer Daves. Author's collection.

mansion where he and his parents had lived since the late 1930s. His father's private library was a time capsule of classic literature, leather-bound scripts, and cultural artifacts from around the world, and the surrounding wooded acreage included the gazebo from Delmer's *A Summer Place* (1959). Jeff Chandler once swam laps in the large pool to impress his girlfriend, Esther Williams.[26]

By 1950, Daves added Westerns to his growing filmography. Following his work on Warner Bros. *Task Force* (1949), a tribute to US aircraft carriers shot in black and white with battle scenes in Technicolor, Daves moved to Twentieth Century-Fox to begin *Broken Arrow*.[27] Daves was essentially a director for hire and was handed *Broken Arrow* as his first assignment at Fox with both script and star in place.[28] The studio had recently concluded a deal with the Music Corporation of America, which included the stipulation that James Stewart star in the screen version of the novel *Blood Brother*.[29] Producer Blaustein, however, leaned heavily toward Daves as director and believed that Fox was "the best place to make the picture." "Zanuck has never pretended anything but enthusiasm for the script," Blaustein wrote, adding that the studio had budgeted $2.3 million for the movie.[30]

Daves relished the opportunity to direct a Western and loved the rigor of working outdoors.[31] He easily related the subject to his own heritage and was able to contribute his emerging directorial style. When he read the script, he recalled that "suddenly my grandfather and all the traditional things that I had heard at his knee came back to me."[32] Above all, Daves wanted to tell the story of American Indians as human beings. He believed that Hollywood had traditionally portrayed Indians as a series of idiots or just plain everyday devils. "We were more daring, I think, than most because we made the supreme devil, the Apache, our hero," he added.[33]

Daves believed that *Broken Arrow* broke the racial barrier by initially indicating that Indians would speak in customary English so the audience could understand them.[34] His concern was that both races not only speak the same language but also sound alike. The movie opens with Tom Jeffords riding across the scenic valley toward the camera, narrating, "What I have to tell happened exactly as you'll see it. The only change will be that when the Apaches speak, they will speak in our language."[35] The film eliminates the broken English and awkward speech patterns of Hollywood Indians and replaces the dialogue with a more conventional style, thus reducing a distinct difference between Apaches and whites. In short, Blaustein said, none of the film's Indians say "Ugh!"[36]

Daves liked to personally supervise the location shots that many filmmakers left to second-unit directors. His camera reinforces a relationship between characters from different backgrounds, often showing a two shot of both Cochise and Jeffords in the same frame to convey a brotherhood of equal status and respect. Other shots place the camera at a low angle below Cochise and Geronimo to emphasize their authority. Additionally, Daves explores human relationships against Sedona's red rock cliffs and skillfully links the protagonist and antagonist in one shot. These scenes are not simply picturesque; they situate characters within their community or landscape without cutting.[37] His boom camera (or crane shot) creates a high vantage point and integrates the characters' movements within the environment. In one scene, the camera moves from the Army's caravan to the cliff high above to show warriors peering down on the vulnerable wagon train. Similarly, toward the end of the movie, miners lead Cochise and Jeffords into a trap with the camera panning from the valley floor to the high cliffs to reveal the white villains secretly waiting in ambush.

The red buttes of Sedona were not the first choice for *Broken Arrow*'s location. Jeffords's opening narration states, "This is the story of a land, of the people who lived on it in the year 1870, and of a man whose name was Cochise."[38] Blaustein wanted to be faithful to that land and to include "as much of the authentic background as practical considerations would allow."[39] The initial meeting between Jeffords, General Howard, and the Apache chief in 1872 actually took place deep within the Dragoon Mountains, twenty-five miles long and one of the so-called sky islands in the Coronado National Forest in Cochise County (southeastern Arizona).[40] The area of the historical meeting, known as China Camp (or China Meadow), is nestled in the West Stronghold Canyon, which rises high above the surrounding valleys and mountains. The site is believed to have

Figure 2.4. China Camp, believed to be the Chiricahua fortress in the West Stronghold Canyon, Dragoon Mountains. Courtesy of Doug Hocking.

once served as a fortress where the Chiricahua could peer unnoticed at approaching enemies far below.[41]

Regardless of its historical significance, the Dragoon Mountains were simply too remote. The terrain's gnarled crevices and jutting, course-grained boulders are surrounded by densely packed grasslands and could easily present a challenge when transporting cast and crew.[42] The studio initially had proposed that "several hundred" Apache extras take up residence in the Dragoons, but Fox terminated all plans to shoot in Cochise County in May 1949.[43] Sedona, however, was a more practical location. Not only was Daves delighted to return to the land of his youthful adventures; he also discovered that Sedona's narrow one-way road had become wide enough for two vehicles.[44] *Broken Arrow* thus offers a bird's-eye view of the scenic Sedona Valley, but the vulnerable location with its exposed Apache dwellings was a far cry from the safety of Cochise's actual fortified camp once nestled high in the Dragoon Mountains.

The red domes of Sedona also provided the setting for Daves's first film shot entirely in color. The nearby Monument Valley boasted its own stark beauty, but the filmmaker was well aware that John Ford had already claimed that landscape as his turf for *Stagecoach* (1939), *Fort Apache* (1948), and *She Wore a Yellow Ribbon* (1949). No other director, including Daves, dared to tread across that Fordian location.[45] Sedona, however, was becoming a favorite site during the postwar years with filmmakers like George Sherman, who had already shot *Comanche Territory* (1950) in stunning Technicolor among its red buttes. Daves himself would stake out Sedona for his subsequent Westerns *Drum Beat* (1954), *The Last Wagon* (1956), and *3:10 to Yuma* (1957).[46] Despite the area's alluring beauty, the filmmaker does not mythologize or romanticize nature or even counterpose it with a corrupt civilization. He instead weaves an organic link between a scene's characters and landscape to create a lyrical emotional power.[47]

Sedona's proximity to two Apache reservations in eastern Arizona also provided the opportunity to employ local Native Americans in the movie. Daves initially made surveys of the San Carlos Reservation as well as the Fort Apache Indian Reservation (home to the White Mountain Apache Tribe), both located in central eastern Arizona approximately two hundred miles from Sedona.[48] San Carlos had offered the agency's superintendent as an intermediary to secure tribal members, but Daves instead chose the White Mountain Apache because they allowed him to work directly with their Tribal Council.[49] The director had shared with the Tribal Council his interest in Apache culture and early experience in Arizona, and his conversation apparently convinced them that their support of a filmed version of Cochise's story would benefit Apache heritage.[50] Fox then transported approximately 250 White Mountain Apache from their home to Sedona, where photography began in June 1949.[51] The studio agreed to pay Apache male riders at $6.60 per eight-hour day and provide accommodations and all meals for two weeks.[52]

Broken Arrow thus employed White Mountain Apache to portray Chiricahua culture. While both tribes share similar ceremonies and are matrilineal, they each have their own distinct traditions and dialect (intermarriage does occur between the two). The White Mountain people are Western Apache, whose reservation is located in the central eastern part of Arizona, and no doubt their proximity to Sedona provided a convenient reason to employ their services. The Chiricahua, on the other hand, reside in New Mexico and Oklahoma, much farther from the film's production site. Ironically, the US Army had once recruited the White Mountain Apache (along with people of San Carlos) to serve as scouts to locate Cochise and later Geronimo.[53]

But absent in the movie are some of the most disturbing events in Chiricahua history. Even though Daves tried to support the Indian point of view, the demands of Hollywood filmmaking meant that he was unable to explore the subsequent tragedy that struck the tribe. *Broken Arrow* concluded in 1872, two years before Cochise died and four years before the United States terminated the Chiricahua Indian Reservation. "We have no desire to indicate the early reservation days, if only because there will be no room in the picture," Blaustein noted.[54] Additionally, the movie's time constraints would not allow for exploring the post-reservation years

(1886–1914) when the US government forcibly removed the Chiricahua from their southwestern homelands and incarcerated a large group—including Geronimo and Cochise's relatives—as prisoners of war in Florida, Alabama, and finally, Oklahoma.[55]

In addition to the White Mountain Apache, Daves hired several Native Americans who completed his vision of Arizona history.[56] Jay Silverheels (1912–1980), who portrayed Geronimo, showed that his versatility reached well beyond his Tonto character in TV's *The Lone Ranger* (1949–1957). The Mohawk actor from Canada's Six Nations of the Grand River Reserve had already attracted attention as the Indian prince who befriends Tyrone Power in *Captain from Castile* (1948). In *Key Largo* (1948), he's a Seminole who arrives in Florida after escaping jail and greets Humphrey Bogart before turning himself over to local law enforcement. *The Lone Ranger* had recently capitulated Silverheels's rise to fame, and his athletic six-foot frame along with his melodious voice easily commanded attention as the bold warrior who breaks with Cochise to form his own band.[57] Additionally, the young Navajo Robert Foster Dover (1934–1995) appeared as the wounded boy Machogee at the beginning of *Broken Arrow*. He had several lines of dialogue with Jeffords and two years later played Geronimo in *Lone Star* (1952).[58]

Another actor, John War Eagle (1901–1977), was Yankton Sioux from South Dakota. He portrayed Nahilzay, Cochise's loyal warrior who is jealous because he wants to wed Sonseeahray. (Nahilzay betrays the Apache chief by attempting to kill Jeffords.) A year later, War Eagle played the Oglala Lakota leader Red Cloud in *Tomahawk* (1951), a character resembling Cochise in *Broken Arrow*. "It is easy for me to put myself in Red Cloud's place," the actor said. "I know how he must have felt when he saw how the tide of events was swinging against his people."[59]

Figure 2.5. Jay Silverheels portrayed Geronimo in *Broken Arrow*. Author's collection.

Other Native actors in *Broken Arrow* joined the cast. Chris Willow Bird (1887–1968) played the spiritual leader Nochalo who presided over Sonseeahray and Jeffords's wedding ceremony. Willow Bird was from the San Ildefonso Pueblo in Santa Fe, New Mexico.[60] The warrior Skinyea was portrayed by Osage actor Charles Leon Soldani (1893–1968), and Cherokee actor William Penn Wilkerson (1902–1966) played the guide Juan who taught Jeffords the Apache language. Wilkerson was also active in politics and previously headed the Republican National Committee on Indian Affairs.[61]

As a former actor, Daves had a knack for drawing credible performances. Michael described his father as "an excellent communicator"

Figure 2.6. William Penn Wilkerson as Juan, who leads Jeffords to the Apache camp. Author's collection.

who had "an understanding of actors of what they needed and what not to do."[62] Daves was apparently "nuts about 'eye' actors" who could project a world of feeling with a flick of their eyelashes. He would squat under the camera lens to study his actors' eyes and became their direct audience contact, a role he cherished with his leading ladies.[63] He also worked well within the studio system and was canny about making sure he had the support of the top people as well as his crew. "He was a collaborator and not a dictator," Michael explained.[64]

But Daves faced challenges when casting Cochise. Although he was willing and wanted to use actual Native Americans for minor characters, the director believed that very few at that time were available for lead roles.

Regardless, he knew he had to seek a strong actor for the Apache chief. "We never considered a star-name for it, either," Daves explained, "because that would have seemed false when all the other actual Indians played scenes with a well-known star obviously not an Indian."[65] Jeff Chandler (1918–1961) was relatively unknown to film audiences and seemed to fit the requirement. The young actor had earned a mild reputation for the radio show *Our Miss Brooks* (1948–1957) and showed his range as a bigoted anti-Indian Army major who shoots and kills the chief's son in *Two Flags West* (1950). For Daves, the casting of Chandler seemed to avoid the possibility of upstaging Native actors and drawing attention to the star himself rather than to the Cochise character.[66] Chandler also seemed to bear some physical resemblance to Cochise, at least according to a historian's description and photographs of Cochise's younger son, Naiche.[67]

Figure 2.7. Jeff Chandler as Cochise. Author's collection.

The tall, slender Brooklyn-born actor, however, needed to "muscle up" to portray a prominent Apache chief. Chandler was prematurely gray and let his own hair grow long, and his Southern California–tanned features served him well in subsequent Westerns and Polynesian adventures. "He needed a couple of months getting the best exercise he could for what would be an acceptable bare-chested Indian," Michael said of Chandler.[68] But Daves was stunned when Chandler's quiet assurance gave way to a loud, bombastic Cochise during the screen test. Stewart, in fact, was startled by the loudmouth actor suddenly shouting in his face. Chandler had read many books on Cochise and assumed that the Apache leader was a commanding figure who brought terror to the West. Daves, on the other hand, wanted Cochise to have a quiet authority, so he took the actor aside to coach him against portraying the "ferocious Indian warrior" stereotype.[69] "My father explained it would be much more effective for Chandler to play it straight and show command without raising his voice," Michael said.[70] After each rehearsal Daves reminded Chandler, "quietly, quietly," so that the chemistry between the actor and Stewart could surface.[71]

Likewise, the studio hoped that newcomer Debra Paget would bypass the usual star syndrome of a Linda Darnell or Loretta Young as an attractive Indian maiden. With the exception of her credits in Fox's tense dramas *Cry of the City* (1948) and *House of Strangers* (1949), Paget was relatively unknown. Zanuck had seen Paget as the dark-haired Italian girl in *Cry of the City* and wanted to avoid a "formula personality" for the role of Sonseeahray.[72] The seventeen-year-old actress seemed to fit his requirement but had to cover her azure blue eyes with painful brown contact lenses and dye her naturally blond hair a raven black. Paget may not have been a recognizable star at the time, but her large eyes and slim figure still recalled the ideal Hollywood Indian maiden. At least one critic remarked

Figure 2.8. Debra Paget as Sonseeahray. Author's collection.

that she looked very much like "a schoolboy's dream of Pocahontas."[73] That same dream became the prototype for Daves's young Native women in his subsequent Westerns.

Broken Arrow offered Daves the opportunity to explore another culture in a serious light. He would later refer to the movie as "the father of the so-called adult Western" and said that it encouraged others to understand Apaches "and all the other American Indians as a result of it."[74] The movie acknowledges cultural diversity by highlighting a few aspects of Apache traditions. One of them, the social dance, is initiated by the woman, and the film shows how it was an informal opportunity for Sonseeahray and Jeffords to become acquainted. Likewise, Juan warns Jeffords to avoid the owl, traditionally a bad omen to the Apache people.[75] But beneath the film's occasional references to Apache culture was a plea for assimilation, or specifically, the forced integration of Indians into white society. As discussed in the previous chapter, the wedding ceremony between Jeffords and Sonseeahray with its fictitious blood sharing and poetic blessing—neither of which are a part of Apache tradition—appeals to Anglo-American expectations. Jeffords may have preferred to marry "according to Apache traditions," but the ceremony itself promotes a white ethnocentric perspective.[76]

Broken Arrow offers the opportunity to explore some real tensions between assimilation versus multiculturalism and its future for Indian/white relations. Ultimately, however, the movie promotes President Grant's Peace Policy and its reservation system as a first step toward forcibly integrating the Apache into the dominant American society. The story takes place from approximately 1869 to 1876, when Grant's policy was designed to assimilate Native Americans—including their education, language, and religion—into white society and break their reliance on tribal lifestyle. In short, the Peace Policy was peaceful only for those tribes who embraced the culture change proposed by agents and missionaries and remained within the boundaries of the reservation.[77]

Scholars have argued that on one level, assimilation was really the government's attempt to colonize and obtain Native land and resources. In fact, assimilation was a method of control to restrict Native movement and undermine and transform their culture.[78] *Broken Arrow*'s vision of peace assumes that the Chiricahua would be confined to a reservation with no ability to migrate to other regions. The Chiricahua were hunters rather than farmers; they lived off the land and moved with the seasons. A loss of Chiricahua nomadic space of hunting and gathering would seriously disrupt seasonal or annual events that depended upon local game and vegetation.[79]

A key scene in *Broken Arrow* actually reveals how the peace plan would gradually erode, rather than preserve, Chiricahua economy and culture. Jeffords, Cochise, and General Howard gather with the Apache to propose a peace treaty to cease all warfare and raiding.[80] Geronimo is opposed to the plan and explains that without the ability to raid into Mexico for corn, blankets, and horses, the Apache would be forced into cattle ranching.[81] "It is not the Apache way to be grandmothers to cattle," he sneers, because traditionally the Chiricahua depended on hunting and raiding, not cattle ranching.[82]

Broken Arrow thus assumes that the Apache must conform to Anglo expectations and accept the conditions of white society. Cochise agrees

Figure 2.9. Sedona location of peace agreement in *Broken Arrow* with Cochise, General Howard, and Jeffords. Author's collection.

Figure 2.10. View of the West Dragoons believed to be near where the actual council meeting of Cochise, General Howard, and Jeffords took place. Author's collection.

to the proposed reservation and advises his warriors to accommodate the encroaching Anglo/European immigration. "Why should not the Apache be able to learn new ways?" he asks, and he explains his decision poetically: "If a big wind comes, the tree must bend or be lifted out by its roots."[83] But Geronimo argues (and is historically proven correct) that Howard's peace proposal will actually open up hundreds of acres of former Chiricahua lands for white appropriation.[84] "Four days ago we were given our territory on a piece of paper. . . . Already our territory is smaller," he points out.[85] Geronimo announces that he is ashamed to be a Chiricahua and rejects Howard's plan, which prompts Cochise to banish the "bad Indian" from the tribe. Daves would repeat the same theme in subsequent films.

Broken Arrow premiered at the Roxy Theater in New York City on July 17, 1950. The premier, however, had been preceded by a July 4 advance screening before approximately four thousand Apache men, women, and children, who had gathered at the Fort Apache Reservation to see themselves portrayed.[86] The movie was a commercial success. *Box Office Report* ranked *Broken Arrow* number seven out of the top fifteen highest-grossing films in 1950 with $3.6 million in domestic revenue.[87] Daves, meanwhile, was determined to remind audiences that his movie was more than just another cowboy-and-Indian Western. In 1951, the Screen Directors Playhouse presented a one-hour radio version of the same story with Daves as writer and Stewart, Chandler, and Paget reprising their roles. Hollywood, said Daves in the show's postscript, needed to correct its depiction of the American Indian as a "purposeless, murdering savage" and restore a "birthright of honor to a brave and proud people."[88]

Based on *Broken Arrow*'s success, Daves and Fox studios reused the same material with slightly different elements and varying outcomes. Meanwhile, the filmmaker continued to explore relations with Indigenous peoples in subsequent films, including non-Westerns. In 1951, he flew cast and crew to Hawaii to film Fox's remake of *Bird of Paradise*. As screenwriter and director, Daves presented *Bird of Paradise* as a Technicolor extravaganza and replicated several of *Broken Arrow*'s key elements. The opening credits include examples of Polynesian signs and religious symbols (similar to *Broken Arrow*'s titles of Apache art) as well as traditions and ceremonial practices. The movie is based on Richard Walton Tully's 1912 play about a doomed romance between a young Caucasian (Louis Jourdan) and a Polynesian beauty (Debra Paget). The film features

Jourdan playing a kind of Jeffords character and Chandler as the refined and college-educated Polynesian similar to Cochise. Once again, the white man marries the virginal Native girl; as in the play and the risqué 1932 film version starring Delores del Río, she leaps into a volcano to save her people. Her sacrifice is similar to Sonseeahray's in *Broken Arrow* whose death brings peace to the southwest.

But Daves actually did explore and even tried to develop a story in which Native culture was actually preferable to white. One of his unfinished projects at Fox, *Daybreak in Bali* (1951), was based on the true story of a young girl raised by a Malay-Muslim foster mother in Malaysia but against her wishes was returned to her Dutch Catholic parents in the Netherlands. The controversial custody battle actually had sparked riots between Malaysia's Muslims and Europeans in 1950.[89] Although the project never developed beyond the initial treatment stage with any script or cast, it shows how Daves, along with his writers and producers, struggled with a progressive story in terms of Native/white relations.[90]

Daybreak in Bali presented several obstacles during a politically sensitive era. Screenwriter Casey Robinson created a treatment that impressed Zanuck, who suggested that Robinson and Daves write the script with Daves as director. In fact, Zanuck believed that the story's interracial theme was a "wonderful follow-up" to *Broken Arrow* and *Bird of Paradise* and should again include Debra Paget. But because of political and cultural concerns—Robinson was worried that Americans might associate an Asian country with the "communism problem"—the studio scrapped the Bali project.[91] Daves himself had doubts that the audience would accept a Balinese versus white cultural conflict, so he subsequently came up with his own "western version" of the story set in the Rocky Mountains during the 1840s. His preliminary treatment shows a white girl separated from her family during an Indian attack on the Army post, but she chooses to remain among the Blackfeet tribe and marries one of their warriors.[92] Fox did not produce either the Bali or Western version, and Daves never returned to a story of a white person "going Native."

The filmmaker's subsequent movies tended to favor Anglo values over ethnic heritage. *Treasure of the Golden Condor* (1953), for example, cleverly circumvents an interracial marriage. Daves loved shooting his movies on foreign locations because he believed they were "an effective way for Hollywood to help spread goodwill throughout the world"[93] For *Treasure of the Golden Condor,* he traveled to Guatemala to photograph the K'iche' Indians (formerly Quiché) along with the historic village of San Antonio Palopó and the Mayan communities of Lake Atitlán.[94]

Daves served as both writer and director for the movie's story about an eighteenth-century French servant (Cornel Wilde) who escapes bondage and travels in search of Mayan treasure. *Treasure of the Golden Condor* is a remake of Fox's *Son of Fury: The Story of Benjamin Blake* (1942) in which a white man (Tyrone Power) ultimately chooses life in the tropical forest with an Indigenous woman (a miscast Gene Tierney) instead of settling in France. *Son of Fury* was based upon Edison Marshall's 1941 novel *Benjamin Blake,* and in his story, the girl dies by suicide. But Zanuck wanted to avoid "sad endings" during a depressing world war, so *Son of Fury* omitted "Tierney's lamentable swim into shark-infested waters."[95]

Eleven years later, *Treasure of the Golden Condor* transforms the Indigenous woman in *Son of Fury* into the Caucasian offspring of a Scottish explorer. Fox struggled with its remake and hired screenwriter Jo Eisinger to draft a revised story in which *Son of Fury*'s Indigenous woman would be rewritten as the wild daughter of the Scotsman and his Inca wife. But Daves thought the story came across as a "taming of the Inca shrew," especially when the white hero kisses the woman and she bites his lip and throws a machete at him. Conversely, she responds with a kiss when the same man twice knocks her down. "What a gal," Daves noted sarcastically, adding that the actress not only would have to act passionately but glower on every page.[96] Zanuck agreed that Eisinger's story had "too much material, too many wild things," before assigning the screenplay to Daves.[97] The result was a sort of compromise in which the daughter (Constance Smith) is European but would wear Indigenous skirts and jewelry to make her look as if she belonged to the Incas.[98]

A year later, Daves's original sympathy for the historical plight of the Apache in *Broken Arrow* appears to wane in his next Western, *Drum Beat* (1954).[99] Both stories again take place during Grant's Peace Policy in which forced Indian assimilation into white society became the proposed solution to Western conflict, and both share similar themes. Daves wrote, directed, and coproduced *Drum Beat* under the banner of Alan Ladd's Jaguar Productions and based his original story on the tragic peace attempt between Modoc and whites. The director relies on his familiar portrayals in *Broken Arrow*, but the film's noble Apache hero has been transformed into the hostile Modoc leader Kintpuash or "Captain Jack" in *Drum Beat*.

Drum Beat continues to preach Native American conformity into white society and reinforces *Broken Arrow*'s message that "good Indians" accept Grant's peace plan while "bad Indians" do not. Historically, the Modoc had been forced from their traditional lands in Tule Lake, northern California, to the Klamath reservation in Oregon in 1864. When the tribe tried to return to Tule Lake, the Modoc War (1872–1873) broke out. *Drum Beat* begins in 1872, when President Grant summons Indian fighter Johnny MacKay (Alan Ladd) to bring peace to the Modoc. Although MacKay's parents were massacred by Indians, he believes that tolerance,

Figure 2.11. On the set of *Drum Beat* with (*from left*) Alan Ladd, Audrey Dalton, Marisa Pavan, and Delmer Daves. Courtesy of the family of Delmer Daves.

and not guns, will bring the Modoc into line. But Captain Jack (a muscular Charles Bronson) instead balks at Grant's peace plan and bolts the reservation. Jack is clearly distinguished from the peaceful Modoc because he speaks broken English and sports a military officer's jacket with shiny brass buttons.

Drum Beat opens with the disclaimer, "The story you are about to see is based upon historical fact. Fictional incidents and characters have been introduced only where necessary to dramatize the truth."[100] The movie returns to the red rocks of Sedona, far from the northern California/Oregon border and Modoc stronghold within its rugged lava beds. Daves again employed the White Mountain Apache as he did in *Broken Arrow*, but here they portray the Modoc. (The actors' Apache attire with headbands and cotton pants tucked in their moccasin boots, however, was a minor historical error.)[101] MacKay shares Jeffords's belief that "war is no good" and that a peace council will resolve Indian/white conflicts.[102] Jack agrees to the talks but instead kills Brigadier General Edward Canby and destroys any hope of peace. "We could've saved a lot of lives," MacKay scolds Jack, "if you hadn't grabbed country that wasn't yours."[103] The Army then executes Jack. As with *Broken Arrow*'s Geronimo and Nahilzay, the recalcitrant Modoc leader must be eliminated so that peace can become possible.[104]

Daves reiterates his point in *Broken Arrow* that a sacrifice of an Indian woman will bring peace to the region. The film's Modoc translator Toby (Marisa Pavan, twin sister to Pier Angeli) looks like Sonseeahray, as both are slender with long black hair tied in pigtails and wear buckskin attire. Toby is sympathetic to MacKay and in love with him, although his romantic interest lies with Nancy Meek (Audrey Dalton), the colonel's daughter. Along with her brother, Manok (Anthony Caruso), Toby believes that Jack is a "bad Modoc" and warns General Canby that the Indian leader plans to kill him.[105] Ultimately, Jack kills Canby and MacKay is wounded. When Toby tries to prevent a Modoc from scalping MacKay, the warrior instead crushes her with a rock.

But the real Toby "Winema" Riddle (1884–1920) actually survived the ambush and saved the life of Alfred B. Meacham, US Superintendent of Indian Affairs for Oregon. He later published a book dedicated to Toby and successfully petitioned Congress to award her a military pension.[106] In an early draft of *Drum Beat*'s script, a Modoc warrior attempts to kill Toby, but she survives. The final screenplay was completed approximately a month later and reveals that Toby instead dies during the ambush.[107]

The movie's tragic ending, although historically inaccurate, reinforces Daves's theme that peace is rarely obtained without bloodshed.

Daves's movies gradually shifted toward a presumption that Native assimilation into white society was an inescapable and even preferable solution. *White Feather* (1955) includes an Indian/white marriage and again opens with the hero's familiar-sounding narration: "What you are about to see actually happened. The only difference will be that when the Indians speak, they will speak in our language so that you can understand them."[108] The white protagonist Josh Tanner (Robert Wagner) serves as a peacemaker between the Cheyenne and the cavalry, and he weds the chief's daughter Appearing Day (Debra Paget, yet again) who with her pigtails and buckskin dress represents Daves's ideal vision of an Indian maiden. In fact, the character's white feather symbolizes "purity" among women of her tribe, which recalls the virginal Sonseeahray in *Broken Arrow*.[109]

In *White Feather*, Daves shared screenplay credit with Leo Townsend, and the movie's Indian/white marriage survives without a tragic ending. But Appearing Day actually prefers white society because she believes that there would be peace and "no more talk of dying." She chooses Josh over her Cheyenne suitor and explains that she's left her people and is now "dead to all of them."[110] Her determination to leave her tribe anticipates the movie's conclusion, in which Tanner narrates that the couple marries and their mixed-blood son ultimately enters the US Military Academy at West Point. *White Feather* finally achieved Daves's vision of an Indian/white union but simultaneously suggested that civilization would absorb Native American autonomy.[111]

White Feather was Daves's only project that offered a lasting romantic union between Natives and whites. His later movies would continue to explore other interracial relationships within a changing postwar society. *Kings Go Forth* (1958) is based on a 1956 novel of same name in which two American soldiers fighting in France during World War II are both in love with Monique, a French-born American woman. In the novel, one of soldiers rejects her because she is "mulatto" (her deceased father was Black and mother white). Monique then commits suicide, and the same soldier later dies in battle.

With *Kings Go Forth*, Daves experimented with the newly revised Production Code of 1956. Although miscegenation between the Black and white races was forbidden by the 1934 Production Code, the revised Code no longer contained any prohibition against these interracial relationships.[112] Daves shows that Monique (Natalie Wood) attempts suicide only when the first soldier (Tony Curtis) rejects her. But she survives to teach in a French orphanage. In the film's conclusion, the second soldier (Frank Sinatra) visits Monique, and the two briefly embrace as the children sing a French rendition of "Under Paris Skies." Producer Frank Ross admitted that he was not in favor of miscegenation but nevertheless supported the movie's interracial love theme. Daves's sentimental union appears inconclusive, but *Variety* noted that for its time, it was hopeful.[113]

Similarly, in *The Badlanders* (1958), Daves explores relations between Mexicans and whites in a fairly upbeat remake of the heist film *The Asphalt Jungle* (1950). *The Badlanders* is set in 1898, when two ex-cons, Peter Van Hoek (Alan Ladd) and John McBain (Ernest Borgnine), are released from the Yuma Territorial Prison and plan to rob a gold mine. McBain risks his life to protect the attractive and kind-hearted Anita (Katy Jurado), a Mexican American woman who rallies the town's inhabitants against the mine's crooked white owners. The two ex-cons ultimately get the gold, and the conclusion again offers the hope of an interracial marriage as Anita joins McBain on his way to Texas. But in *Cowboy* (1958), Daves denies any possibility of a Mexican/white union when a love match between a hotel clerk-turned-cattle wrangler (Jack Lemmon) and a Mexican woman (Anna Kashfi) is forbidden by her wealthy and class-conscious father, who explains, "Our way of life is too different from yours."[114]

Daves's final Indian-themed Western, *The Last Wagon* (1956), is again based on the assumption that civilization is preferable to life in the wilderness. Daves cowrote and directed the movie in which the protagonist. Comanche Todd (Richard Widmark), is a white man raised by the Comanche, marries one of their women, and has two sons. But when his family is brutally murdered by four white men, he hunts them down one by one. He stumbles onto a wagon train, and while the young people are away swimming, the rival Apache raid the campsite and kill all the adults except Todd. As a "half-wild white man raised by Indians"—according to Fox publicity—Todd cleverly eliminates his Apache opponents and relies on his Comanche survival tactics to guide six young people safely through Apache territory.[115] He's further "redeemed" by explaining to the judge—the General Howard character from *Broken Arrow*—that he killed the four men in retaliation for his own family's murder. Ultimately, the judge grants custody of Todd to the attractive and refined female passenger Jenny (Felicia Farr), so the half-wild white man will return to society and become civilized.

Daves toned down some of *The Last Wagon*'s original story by Gwen Bagni Gielgud. The author's protagonist is a white man and former river pilot who meets up with a wagon train that includes a wealthy Louisianan and his snooty daughter, Valinda. Bonchance, their "wild and primitive" Cajun servant, shocks the lily-white passengers when she writhes during a voodoo incantation then snaps off a chicken head and offers its bloody heart to a pagan altar.[116] Daves wasn't about to include exotic pagan rituals among a wagonload of youngsters, so he reworked Bonchance into Valinda's attractive and more "refined" Navajo half-sister Jolie. The elegant and well-groomed Jolie (Susan Kohner) represents the ideal assimilated Native within white society; her manners and generosity serve as a stark contrast to Valinda's racist anti-Indian remarks. But the movie delivers a lesson on tolerance when the Navajo woman eventually transforms the bigoted white. Valinda, who barely survives a rattlesnake bite, later becomes indebted to her half-sister for saving her life and helping her "grow up."[117]

Daves directed his last Western *The Hanging Tree* in 1959. The prolific filmmaker suffered a series of heart attacks around that time, and his

Figure 2.12. Jolie (Susan Kohner), foreground, is the attractive and more "refined" Navajo half-sister in *The Last Wagon*. Courtesy the family of Delmer Daves.

ailing health confined him to assignments that were physically less challenging than Westerns.[118] He thus turned to several weepy melodramas—which his son Michael coined "parlor, bedroom, and bath" films—and while he still traveled, the demands of location shooting for Westerns had become too strenuous and jeopardized his health. Daves loved Westerns and missed the rugged outdoors. "But he had to hide his illness," Michael explained. "He was worried that the studios would not hire him if they found out."[119]

Daves's preference for socially progressive Westerns thus gave way to several melodramas for Warner Bros. that exposed the hypocrisy of middle- and upper-class American society. A few critics tended to dismiss them as "good old-fashioned tearjerkers for the feminine trade," while others noted that his stories had shifted from the Hawks-Ford realism of the masculine action movie to the Sirk-Minnelli axis of so-called women's pictures.[120] "That part of his career was really based on what he could do," Michael explained.[121] In 1959 Daves wrote, directed, and produced *A Summer Place*, his first in a series of melodramas that suggested that teenage sex was natural and even healthy. The *New York Times* later credited the film for helping to "redefine the way sex was portrayed in American movies."[122] Daves explored similar themes in subsequent films; *Susan Slade* (1961) included attempted suicide and a teen pregnancy, *Parrish* (1961) showed a generational conflict and another teen pregnancy, *Rome Adventure* (1962) featured a forbidden romance (and Emilio Pericoli's unforgettable rendition of the song "Al di là"), and "*Youngblood Hawke*" (1964) revealed adultery and seduction within the publishing industry. His final film was *The Battle of the Villa Fiorita* (1965), an uneven story of adultery and spoiled children who descend on an illicit liaison.

Yet the racial portrayals that Daves once depicted as ideals of postwar

Figure 2.13. Jeff Chandler, Debra Paget, Delmer Daves, James Stewart, and crew members on the set of *Broken Arrow.* Courtesy of the family of Delmer Daves.

liberalism took a back seat to his progressive sexual themes. His Black, Native, and Asian characters now emerged as the different "Other" in keeping with their prewar social and subservient status. In *The Hanging Tree,* a penniless prospector who sells his cabin and for a five-dollar gold piece offers to throw in his plump and jovial Native American servant with braided pigtails. (She obediently jumps when he beckons and totes his belongings on her back.) The wealthy white patriarch in *Susan Slade* reminds his friends that his submissive and smiling Japanese female servant "can cook, too."[123] In *Parrish,* Blacks join whites in the tobacco fields and sing spirituals recalling the antebellum era, and in *Youngblood Hawke,* the only Black character is relegated to the role of a security guard. Even the brief appearance of Barbara McNair singing the national anthem in Daves's *Spencer's Mountain* (1963) seemed only a symbolic nod to Black performers.[124]

Regardless of his later racial portraitures, Daves had helped lay the foundation for Indian reform in Hollywood Westerns. *Broken Arrow* demonstrated that Indians and whites could stand side by side as "brothers" within an evolving postwar society and showed that no real basis exists for treating one race as inherently different from, and hence inferior to, another.[125] Paradoxically, Daves promoted Apache ceremonies and traditions while he simultaneously created model Native American characters who would uphold the values of white society. His movie's plea for racial tolerance would ultimately provide a precedent for many Hollywood Westerns. But *Broken Arrow* was released during an era in which the federal government's drastic program of forced assimilation meant the loss of treaty land as well as Native identity and culture. For a while, the screen's Native Americans survived only by compromising their heritage.

3 | Promoting Postwar Tolerance

Broken Arrow's release in 1950 coincided with the intensifying federal efforts to implement assimilationist policies. From 1940 to 1950 Congress had passed a number of laws, and the federal government issued a report proposing the integration of Native people into mainstream society. By 1953, Termination became official and would end federal treaty obligations to Indian tribes and eradicate tribal governments and politically autonomous reservations. The ultimate goal was to strip tribes of their culture and traditions and definitively absorb Indians into the dominant white society, erasing tribal status and eliminating their special wardship with the federal government.[1] Daves's film hardly proposed eliminating reservations and eradicating tribal governments. But whether intentional or not, the movie's underlying theme reinforces the belief that Native Americans must adopt white Anglo values to survive.

Broken Arrow was arguably the first major Hollywood Western to at least hint at these problematic Indian policies. The story's underlying message that Indians—and not whites—would eventually have to compromise their identity established the foundation for subsequent Westerns that extoled the virtues of assimilation at the expense of preserving Native culture (see further discussion in chapter 4). Assimilation itself was nothing new in US history; the film's version of the Peace Policy under President Grant showed that the Apache were forced from their ancestral homes and onto reservations. But the federal government continued to push their agenda with its Code of Indian Offences in 1883 that restricted the cultural and religious ceremonies of Native people. The notorious boarding school system had absorbed Native youth into white society through education and eradication of their culture. And the Dawes Act of 1887 (also called the General Allotment Act) further subdivided reservation lands into individual plots in hopes that farming would end the old communal way of life and turn American Indians into private-property owners. Likewise, Termination and its companion "relocation program" would move unemployed Indians into urban areas and prepare them for mainstream conversion.[2]

During this midcentury era of evolving postwar Indian policies, Twentieth Century-Fox created press material that played up *Broken Arrow*'s theme of interracial cooperation and friendship. While no evidence exists that Fox was specifically responding to federal Indian policies, the movie's advertising reinforced that its noble Indians would embody white society's ideals of justice and racial tolerance. The studio's team of spin doctors, headed by Hollywood press agent Harry Brand, sought to deploy the Jeffords/Cochise friendship as a model of America's race relations. Brand was the studio's head of publicity from 1935 to his retirement in 1962 (although he still continued as a consultant), and he was a master of public relations in the age of gossip magazines. He had steered the PR campaigns of Shirley Temple, Alice Faye, Ronald Colman, and Rita Hayworth and diligently fed celebrity stories to the media. One of Brand's notorious clients was the portly silent film comedian Fatty Arbuckle, whose arrest for the alleged rape and murder of model Virginia Rappe in 1921 created a firestorm of controversy and a big headache for his publicist.[3]

Press Pass
TO PUBLICITY DEPARTMENT
TWENTIETH CENTURY-FOX FILM CORPORATION
BEVERLY HILLS, CALIFORNIA
NAME DON BRINN
REPRESENTING WIDE WORLD PHOTOS
VALID UNTIL DECEMBER 31, 1949
STUDIO PUBLICITY MANAGER HARRY BRAND
351
THIS PASS NOT VALID UNLESS SIGNED BY THE HOLDER ON THE REVERSE SIDE

Figure 3.1. Fox press pass by Harry Brand. Courtesy of Marc Wanamaker / Bison Archives.

Brand and his team went to work. They created multiple advertising tools for *Broken Arrow* ranging from posters and lobby cards to interviews and production stories. The movie's theme of a universal brotherhood sprang from Arnold's novel and guided Maltz's screenplay and would therefore shape its advertising campaign. The film's posters were key during a troubled postwar era because they emphasized how two sworn enemies developed a friendship and demonstrated that Indians and whites could live together peacefully. To that end, Fox made sure that its advertising slogans and vivid illustrations conveyed that the Cochise/ Jeffords friendship would break down the walls of social bigotry and serve as a model for Indian/white tolerance. These ads thus offered the

Figure 3.2. Advertising poster for *Broken Arrow* showing Cochise and Jeffords (holding Sonseeahray) fighting common enemies. Courtesy of FilmAffinity.

reminder that Daves's film was "truly reflective of the American traditions of justice, tolerance, and dignity for all men."[4] From the studio's perspective, America's viewers would grasp the movie's moral lesson: "These were men who might have killed one another, but instead . . . developed a deep and true friendship that served as a practical basis for reform of then existing Indian-white inequities."[5]

While *Broken Arrow* extolled the virtues of white society, it simultaneously attempted to entice potential audience members with its own version of Native American culture. The film created that culture from a point of view that reinforced white Anglo values. By promoting the film as "based on actual fact," Fox was hoping to use details about Apache tradition to lure patrons into theaters. Many ads emphasized Apache culture and offered theater exhibitors various "lines"—supposedly of factual nature—that would playfully engage curious viewers. For example, "Did you know that Apaches solved the mother-in-law problem beautifully—no man was ever allowed to talk or even to see his wife's mother?" Or, "An Apache girl is presumed to have reached the marriageable age at 13?" One ad stated that "Apaches were the best all-around warriors of American Indians," which was sure to excite any fan of cowboy-and-Indian adventures. Others catered to white Anglo romantic ideals by falsely claiming that when the index fingers of both bride and groom are cut and tied together in the wedding scene, it was indeed an "old Apache marriage" ceremonial tradition.[6]

In its efforts to attract young patrons, Fox created a few activities packaged as educational that recalled romantic tales of America's Natives. Various gimmicks ranged from teaching youngsters how to interpret the puffs of Indian smoke signals to advising civic groups on how to build huge bonfires with the help of the Boy Scouts and Camp Fire Girls. Other suggestions promoted a frontiersman and Indian girl costume contest and lessons in archery.[7] The studio further publicized the movie by sending five Native Americans on a two-week tour of RKO theaters in New York. An attractive Native American lecturer, Princess Yellow Bird, spoke to women's groups and movie critics to assert (erroneously) that *Broken Arrow* was the first Hollywood film to deal sympathetically with American Indians.[8]

Additional materials maximized or exaggerated the actors' various adventures and risks on location. Production trivia thus pointed out that

Stewart did not use a double for the scene in which his head was outlined by steel-tipped arrows against a tree and that Paget's brown contact lenses exploded under intense lamp heat and the actress reportedly "almost drowned" while swimming. Other anecdotes attempted to contrast Indian and white attitudes, as when an Apache actor advised Stewart that the star's idle chatter spoiled the scenic view. In another incident, an Apache "medicine man" criticized how whites moved too rapidly from the desert heat to air-conditioned bungalows. Such extremes in temperature, he pointed out, were the best way to get sick.[9]

But at the center of *Broken Arrow*'s poster campaign was the interracial love story. These ads targeted a potential female audience and held out the promise that the price of a ticket would offer sensuality and romance.[10] Many posters depicted the handsome white man embracing the sexy Indian maiden, which the studio cleverly tailored to play as a kind of antidote to social ills. One ad showed the attractive Sonseeahray in the arms of Jeffords with the words "the powerful and unusual story of a white man's love for an Indian girl, that shattered the barriers of color and hate."[11] While *Broken Arrow*'s marriage between Jeffords and Sonseeahray does not survive to the end of the film, subsequent Westerns would show a lasting relationship with the Native girl (or occasionally the Native man) joining white society.

Beyond all the studio hype, Fox hoped that *Broken Arrow* would become an example promoting international understanding and world peace. In that sense, the story's message of peace and brotherhood was in sharp contrast to *Unconquered*, a 1947 allegory of Cold War politics that became Paramount's fitting analogy to the present communist purge. The Gary Cooper and Paulette Goddard adventure was produced and directed by the redoubtable Cecil B. DeMille, known for his outspoken right-wing views during an era of labor strife and anti-communist propaganda. Set in the eighteenth-century American wilderness, *Unconquered*'s opening narration praises those who "push ever forward the frontiers of man's freedom."[12] The obstacles to this freedom were the Ottawa chief Pontiac and his Indian allies, determined to abort British encroachment and restore French ascendancy in the West.

The advertising campaign for DeMille's film, needless to say, was a far cry from *Broken Arrow*'s theme of brotherly love and international understanding. The filmmakers behind *Unconquered* instead conflated Pontiac's rebellion with the postwar communist scare. Beneath its anti-communist rhetoric, *Unconquered* hinted that a person's "Indianness" was politically risky during the Cold War era. "America today resists red ideas as it once resisted Red Indians in the pioneer days of *Unconquered*," touted the movie's pressbook.[13] Paramount's advertising slogan further reinforced the desire to snuff out communists, with an eagle's outstretched wings and the words "Keep America Conquered" across its silhouette.[14]

But three years later, the more politically progressive Darryl Zanuck at Fox preferred to publicize Daves's movie as ideal propaganda for world peace. The story's theme that two sworn enemies could find a common ground within a troubled world also coincided with America's newly established role in the United Nations. Both the UN and Hollywood were eager to sell American values at home and abroad, and Fox cooperated by advising newspapers and clergy members to speak of its pacifist theme as an antidote to prevailing political tensions. "In an age when another war spells impending doom for millions of people," *Broken Arrow*'s pressbook preached, "we too must learn how to break the arrow, how to live in peace with the rest of the world."[15] *Broken Arrow* opened the same year that a UNESCO proposal called for the distribution of a film that would promote human rights. Daves's Western emerged as an obvious allegory. In 1951, the Golden Globes Awards named *Broken Arrow* as the "Best Film Promoting International Understanding."[16]

But even before reviewers aired their opinions, Zanuck had looked closely at the final print of *Broken Arrow* just before its August 1950 release. In spite of his confidence that the movie would be an important milestone in changing Native/white relations, at a late stage he expressed uncertainty about the strength of the film's narrative. In one of his lengthy memos, dated about a month before the film's opening and long after the extensive post-production process, Zanuck pointed out a few errors or "excesses" and advised Daves to avoid repeating them with his next production, *Bird of Paradise*. The studio head noted that the tempo in *Broken Arrow*'s dialogue was "hopelessly slow" and that the camera was "lost at times" with uneven angles. "I have just looked at a report of the amount of film shot on this picture," he declared, "and it is far in excess of any other Technicolor picture in the history of this company."[17] His advice to Daves was to cut down on his movies' seemingly unending sequences of slow dialogue. After all, Zanuck explained, he only wanted *Bird of Paradise* to be a better picture than *Broken Arrow* and to be made more "efficiently and effectively."[18]

Despite *Broken Arrow*'s lengthy passages and slow dialogue, many reviewers reiterated the movie's campaign for an understanding between two races. An early review appeared in the *Tucson Star Citizen*, not far from where the story of Cochise and Jeffords actually took place. The writer praised Stewart's simple, drawling portrayal of Tom Jeffords along with Chandler's speech that was a relief from the grunts, "How's," and malevolent leers of past movie Indians. He added that while Chandler did not create a believable Cochise, the actor was in complete sympathy with Arnold's interpretation. The writer boasted that a preview audience of more than one hundred cast not one negative vote.[19]

Other news outlets picked up the film's sympathy toward the Apache. *The New Republic* observed that "the days when the only good Indian was as a dead Indian are definitely over in Hollywood" and noted that the industry apparently displayed a "reformed attitude" toward American Indians. The article's comments that the film made "fitting amends, though a little belated" and held a "decent regard for history" were echoed by other publications as well. *The Rotarian* remarked that *Broken Arrow* was something new for a Western and was "interesting in its presentation of Indians as individuals with mores worthy of respect." *Newsweek* agreed, adding that Daves's story provided a shopworn theme with a refreshingly new twist. The *Christian Century,* noting the respectable portrayal of Indians, paralleled *Broken Arrow*'s racial theme with contemporary conflicts when it praised the film as "a persuasive argument for sanity in time of hostilities."[20]

Philip Hartung, writing for the liberal Catholic magazine *Commonweal,* also pointed out that *Broken Arrow* was part of the postwar cycle that included Westerns as vehicles for liberal ideals. He compared the movie's theme of racial and political coexistence to that of *Pinky, Home of the Brave,* and *Lost Boundaries,* all of which dealt with contemporary Black/white attitudes. *Broken Arrow,* he argued, devoted the same serious attention to the race question while advocating that white society stand alongside its Native people. Hartung conceded that the film oversimplified the issues but added that it nonetheless illustrated the racial problem from both sides. Just treating the movie's Indians as real people and not as symbols of a painted menace, he explained, was a definite step forward.[21]

But a small faction of critics dismissed any suggestions that the movie promoted interracial harmony. The weekly magazine the *New Yorker* instead described *Broken Arrow* as a "bland bubble" that might be a pleasant way to waste a couple of summer hours. *Time* magazine pointed out that while Daves's film painted a dignified portrait of American Indians, its love story strained its sense of realism.[22] The most acerbic comments came from Bosley Crowther of the *New York Times* who called out *Broken Arrow*'s patronizing attempt to "anglicize" its Indians. Crowther complained that Daves, in his enthusiasm to treat the Indian with politeness and respect, instead "brought forth red men who act like denizens of the musical comedy stage." The Princeton-educated critic was recognized at the time as the country's most influential commentator of motion pictures and enjoyed debunking Hollywood's movies. In addition to criticizing Chandler's self-righteous demeanor, he described Paget as a "China-doll" who engaged in downright embarrassing "gitchy-goo love-making" with Stewart. Crowther ultimately dismissed the picture as a reasonable account of American Indians, adding "they merit justice, but not such patronage."[23]

Noted *Los Angeles Time*'s movie critic Philip K. Scheuer took a stance quite opposite from that of Crowther. Scheuer agreed that the American Indian's image traditionally had been difficult to capture on the screen. But for him, *Broken Arrow* was "of such beauty and enduring spirit" that he desired to "live through it a second time" and advised his readers to do the same. In contrast to Crowther's mockery, Scheuer praised the performances of Chandler, Stewart, and Paget, who "somehow attained dignity without stuffiness."[24]

Despite Crowther's history of destroying a film that he considered inferior with a scathing review, industry trade newspapers had spotted a winner. *Daily Variety* trumpeted that *Broken Arrow* displayed "top-rank efforts" and was "geared to garner heavy grosses." The *Independent Exhibitors Film Bulletin* agreed that the film would "undoubtably reap a rich harvest at the box office." Others noted the movie's potential to reach a broad audience. New York's weekly *Harrison's Reports* labelled *Broken Arrow* as "excellent for the family" and "should satisfy all types of patrons, western fans or not." Fox was especially pleased with the endorsement of Will Rogers Jr., who proclaimed the film "the greatest motion picture ever produced about Indians' relations with white men."[25]

African American newspapers seized the opportunity to compare the Indians' plight to Black/white racial injustice. These newspapers ran ads that encouraged Blacks to identify with other marginalized people revolting against those same forces that oppressed them. The advertisement with Jeffords embracing Sonseeahray that appeared in *Ebony*, the monthly Afro-American magazine founded in 1945, was specifically tailored to Black interest. Its caption, "Nothing can change our love—neither the color of your skin, nor mine," foregrounded an endorsement by NAACP executive secretary Walter White.[26]

Other Black newspapers applied the same egalitarian approach. The *Los Angeles Sentinel* described *Broken Arrow* as "one of the strongest indictments of racial misunderstanding the screen has yet offered," and *The Baltimore Afro-American* pointed out that the Indians are "shown to be men like all others." Additionally, the movie's marriage between Sonseeahray and Jeffords prompted the *Chicago Defender* to praise the screen's "new treatment" of this subject and to hint that Hollywood should take another look at the Production Code's prohibition of Black/white miscegenation. The reviewer also reminded readers that when a white man in the film referred to Jeffords as "an Indian lover," similar denunciations had been hurled by bigots toward "friends of the Negro."[27]

Figure 3.3. Sonseeahray's pigtails recalled tiresome clichés of Hollywood's Native Americans. Author's collection.

Rather than focus on racial injustice, a few Native Americans pointed to the movie's problematic portrayals of their tradition and culture. Amelia Naiche, daughter of Cochise's younger son, Naiche, and his second wife, Haozinne, was not impressed. She believed that Jeff Chandler "lacked the dignity and bearing of a chief."[28] Years later, Naomi Hartford of the Fort Sill Apache in Oklahoma declared that just about everything was wrong with the movie. For her, obvious mistakes like the Western Apache feathers and Sonseeahray's pigtails recalled tiresome clichés of Hollywood's Native Americans.[29]

On the other hand, anthropologist Trudy Griffin-Pierce believed that Chandler's Cochise provided a positive role model. Griffin-Pierce said she was part Catawba Indian from South Carolina and was only four years old when she read Arnold's novel. She had grown up with many kids asking why she "looked so different" with her dark, almond-shaped eyes and high cheekbones, and the movie had helped her accept her own Native identity. "Cochise's dignity, integrity, and stature as a great leader," she explained, "remained etched in my mind despite the great liberties that I later learned were taken with his story."[30] One of those liberties, *Broken Arrow*'s unrealistic portrayal of Sonseeahray's Puberty Rite, Griffin-Pierce had praised for its careful attention to detail.[31]

But James Kunestsis brushed off any suggestion that *Broken Arrow*'s Puberty Rite was accurate. Kunestsis, whose ancestors had been prisoners of war in Florida during the Chiricahua removal in 1886, pointed out that the movie had substituted the White Mountain Apache ceremonial

Figure 3.4. Sonseeahray's fanlike headdress had nothing to do with Chiricahua Apache culture. Author's collection.

traditions for the Chiricahua's.[32] "Some of the older folks say that's a good movie for kids to see, but it's not accurate. We know and still know that the Apaches are White Mountain," he said.[33] Kunestsis easily spotted other errors and laughed. Sonseeahray's large, flat, fan-like headdress, for example, had nothing to do with Chiricahua or any Apache tribe. "In Apache culture, she does not wear a headdress. None of the Apache tribes do that," he explained. "There's a split in genders. Only men wear it. Even our own kids knew it was fake."[34]

Meanwhile, Cherokee scholar Liza Black took a close look at *Broken Arrow*'s press materials. The movie's behind-the-scenes stories, labelled as "ballyhoo," included attention-getting anecdotes and publicity stunts about the film to playfully engage the viewer. These stories may even have been fabricated, but Black nonetheless pointed out that absent any cultural context, the publicity came across as both patronizing and even sexist. A studio press release, for example, compared Stewart's marriage to Sonseeahray with an "actual" proposal for the actor's arranged marriage by a Jess Thunder Cloud. Apparently, Thunder Cloud knew that Stewart was single and thus offered his own fifteen-year-old daughter in exchange for three horses and a cow. Stewart playfully responded that he lacked the necessary livestock.[35] No doubt the anecdote intended to be humorous to a 1950s audience, but Black instead saw an insidious message that actually condoned bartering over a Native girl's body.[36]

Nevertheless, during the early 1950s, several organizations, including the Association of American Indian Affairs, lavished praise on *Broken Arrow*. The nonprofit group, which at that time boasted affluent non-Native members, was established in 1922 and advocated to protect Indian culture and sovereignty. The Association recommended the movie for "it's bold, honest treatment of Indian history" and took one step further by announcing that the film proved that American Indians must be considered first-class citizens.[37] As an advocacy group for Native Americans, the Association adopted a white progressive point of view and complimented the movie for discarding traditional Hollywood stereotypes. Noted anthropologist and author Oliver La Farge was then serving as the Association's president and had received the Pulitzer Prize for his 1929 novel *Laughing Boy*. His book told the story of the clash between Navajo and white cultures that ends tragically. In 1934, Metro-Goldwyn-Mayer turned *Laughing Boy* into the little-known movie of the same title starring matinee idol Ramón Novarro and a seductive Lupe Vélez. The film's theme of civilization's corruption of Native culture was suitable for liberals and reformers who, like La Farge, had been lamenting the Indian's plight. But for all its noble intentions, *Laughing Boy* was a box-office flop.[38]

La Farge was pleased with *Broken Arrow* and saw its financial potential. The Association's National Film Committee described *Broken Arrow* as "one of the first movies since *The Vanishing American* to attempt a serious portrayal of the Indian side" of American history. Movies like this are needed, LaFarge explained, because decades of stereotyping have prejudiced Americans against Indians and strengthened discrimination. LaFarge, basking in the movie's enthusiastic reception, announced that the press from coast to coast credited the "new Hollywood approach toward the American Indian" to the Association's efforts.[39]

The Association continued to trumpet *Broken Arrow* as a herald of racial reform at a private screening in New York City. The organization called on its members and guests to recognize the Indian "as a human member of the human race" and products of environmental violence rather than symbols of ferociousness. The Association added, rather apologetically, that while the movie reminded the audience that the Apache were the "most deeply-feared and most truculent of all Western Indians," they still shared very understandable human emotions of filial relationships and a comprehension of fair play. Torture and bloodshed were not always instigated by the Indians because broken promises of white men also led to violence, the organization explained in its uneasy attempt to balance the scales of history.[40]

At the same screening, the Association's vice president, Eduard Lindeman, explained that the National Film Committee encouraged producers to tell the truth about America's Natives. *Broken Arrow* is an "effort too long postponed," Lindeman said, reiterating that it's the "only film produced which strives to seek an authentic portrayal of American Indians."[41] The committee believed that authenticity was the best guarantor of artistic success but raised no objection to dramatic rearrangement of people and events as long as depictions of history did not defame American Indians.[42] Plans included formalized relations with the Motion Picture Association of America and the Society of Independent Producers. Lindeman closed his remarks with a plea for financial support for the Association.[43]

But by the 1950s, US Indian policy, which had previously favored tribal self-government, increasingly promoted a more "homogenized society." The result was less federal aid and services to tribes and instead new efforts that forcibly pushed Indians into white society. The Association—once the nemesis of Federal Termination policies—thus faced headwinds in public opinion and responded by leaning in a more conservative direction. Rather than support Native sovereignty and culture, the Association began to hint at the Indians' new role in American society, which they believed would accord them the same opportunities as whites and ultimately lead to assimilation.[44]

Long-time president La Farge, formerly the champion for American

Indian rights, did an about face and favored Federal Termination. "Indians must become absorbed into the general population," he announced and further warned that "they may or may not be able to retain enriching elements of their own culture." His outlook was especially pessimistic for the future of Native American autonomy and sovereignty. "We do know as an unescapable fact," he continued, "that no minority of 400,000 can survive among 150,000,000 of another culture, and retain its identity forever."[45] In spite of its plea for cultural and racial tolerance, a film like *Broken Arrow*, with its strong overtones of Indian compromise, was in line with the prevailing opinion that assimilation was emerging as a "solution" to Native American survival.

Subsequent Westerns would reinforce the assumption that Native Americans must adapt to white society. Even the movies' artwork followed suit. A poster for Daves's later Western, *The Last Wagon* (1956), showed a row of Indians along a ridge peering down at a wagon rolling through the desert. The accompanying slogan that "nothing could stop the last wagon from coming through" is a celebration of civilization's encroachment. Stories of Indian/white romances also advocated that white society was a desired goal. *White Feather*'s (1955) advertisement showed Josh Tanner embracing Appearing Day while an angry warrior in the background brandishes a knife. The underlying message is that the white man will rescue the Native woman from her tribe and ultimately introduce her to civilization. (In the movie, Appearing Day rejects her heritage when she marries Tanner.)

Assimilation—under the guise of Christian charity—also became cinema's solution to hostile Indian/white relations. In *Walk the Proud Land* (1956), federal Indian agent Audie Murphy proudly strolls across the vast frontier with a forceful reminder that "his [Christian] faith built a fortress in a wilderness of hate!" The message was even more pronounced with the poster for *Pillars of the Sky* (1956); while Indians and cavalry fight in the background, the words "This was the night of the tomahawk and the cross" are splashed across the top. *Broken Arrow* offered a more subtle solution to Indian/white tensions, but subsequent 1950s Westerns would preach that conformity to white society was the answer to the frontier's problematic relations.

4 | Post *Broken Arrow*

The popularity of *Broken Arrow* initially encouraged a trend of pro-Indian Westerns. One of them, *Chief Crazy Horse* (1955), cast Natives in a sympathetic light and purportedly told the "Indians' side" of the infamous battles between the Sioux and the US Army. "There is a vogue for Indian pictures right now and this is an Indian picture, so it should do all right at the box office," observed the *Hollywood Reporter*.[1] Other postwar Westerns had already departed from the cowboy-and-Indian formula by reinventing history's white heroes. *Sitting Bull*, for example, portrayed Custer "not as prettily as in the past, but more realistically as a demented colonel" with an egotistical disregard for orders.[2]

The trend toward sympathetic Indian portrayals continued well into the late 1950s. A study of fifty-one postwar Westerns from 1946 to 1959 revealed that almost half, or twenty-four, were actually pro-Indian or included positive portrayals of significant Native American characters.[3] These successors to Daves's film usually preached the same theme of racial tolerance as a desired goal toward eliminating social injustice and inequality. But along with mutual coexistence, many of these movies favored forced assimilation as a way of obtaining a long-term solution to Indian/white tensions on the frontier. Hollywood filmmakers thus attempted to "anglicize" their Native heroes in films that were both narratively and thematically similar to *Broken Arrow*. *The Battle at Apache Pass, Taza, Son of Cochise, Sitting Bull, Tomahawk,* and *Apachè* are examples of 1950s Westerns whose message of assimilation underlies their stories of Indian/white friendships.

Jeff Chandler's Cochise inspired Hollywood's noble Indian leader and the type became a staple in many postwar Westerns. Chandler duplicated his role as Cochise in Universal's *The Battle at Apache Pass* (1952), which recreated the Bascom affair that occurred many years before Jeffords's meeting with the Apache chief. Although the tragic 1861 event had sparked eleven years of Apache/white conflict, *The Battle at Apache Pass* instead offers a kind of contrived peace between both the Army and the Chiricahua. Cochise and an Army major both want peace; others, namely Bascom (John Hudson) and Geronimo (Jay Silverheels), believe that fighting is the only solution to racial problems. (The movie falsely blames Geronimo for kidnapping the boy.) The theme of a few individuals battling a prejudiced society reappears: A major's efforts to negotiate with Cochise are met with angered resistance from his officers. But the Army's use of the powerful Howitzer cannons at a mountain pass were previously unknown to Cochise and signaled that ultimately Apaches must reconcile to white demands. The film's conclusion thus suggests that Apaches are forced to surrender as Cochise loses men against the military and his wife is seriously injured in the same battle.[4]

Chandler again appeared briefly as the noble Apache leader in Douglas Sirk's *Taza, Son of Cochise* (1954), which offered the same theme of a peaceful coexistence as its predecessors. In this movie Taza is reinvented as a hero when he abandons some of his own heritage and conforms to white culture. The story immediately follows Cochise's death, when the

Figure 4.1. Poster for *The Battle at Apache Pass*. Courtesy of Wikipedia.

dying chief had asked his two sons to follow his teachings. One of the sons, Taza (Rock Hudson), works to achieve the same sort of ideal peace as his father. But the other son Naiche (Rex Reason) and Geronimo (Ian MacDonald), who believes that peace will die with Cochise, harshly resist. Taza even agrees to settle the Apache on the San Carlos Reservation but his adoption of white civilization (he dons a military uniform to patrol the Indians) causes much criticism among his own people. Ultimately, Taza must kill his own brother and ask the Army to relocate Geronimo to some eastern reservation before admitting that peace is finally possible.

With *Taza, Son of Cochise,* the studio took great artistic license to dramatize the efforts toward assimilation. Historically, Taza did not kill his younger brother Naiche; Taza was part of an Apache delegation sent to Washington, DC, and fell ill and died in 1876. Naiche then became the final hereditary chief of the Chiricahua but later joined Geronimo's revolt.[5]

Both *The Battle at Apache Pass* and *Taza, Son of Cochise* proposed white society's version of mutual cooperation as a way to achieve Indian/white unity. Other fifties Westerns followed suit with their Indian heroes adopting a white peace plan. Although sympathetic, *Sitting Bull* (1954) riled critics with its many liberties in its story of the great Hunkpapa Lakota medicine man (J. Carrol Naish). "And, at the end of this crazy horse opera," scoffed the *New York Times*, "we are led to believe that Grant and Sitting Bull agree on a policy of co-existence between the white men and the red!"[6] *Sitting Bull* became another example of studio artistic license; historically, he had fled to Canada to escape the Army's wrath and was killed by Indian agency police in 1890.

Universal's *Tomahawk* (1951) all but whitewashed the tragic history between the Sioux and the US government. The story appeared to resemble *Broken Arrow* with a white man (Van Heflin) acting as a peacemaker between the Sioux and the Army. *Tomahawk* opens with an 1866 peace conference in the Dakota Territory between the US cavalry and the Sioux chief Red Cloud (John War Eagle).[7] The problem, according to the *New York Times*, was that the movie's depiction of history was "hopelessly fuzzy."[8] The rather ambiguous conclusion suggests that the Fort Laramie Treaty of 1868, which set aside the sacred Black Hills as a part of the Great Sioux Reservation, was a long-term victory for the Sioux. "From this day forward, all war between the parties of this agreement shall forever cease," the movie's narrator explains, adding "for another 30 years the sun will continue to rise on the world of the Sioux."[9]

But the fate of the Great Sioux Reservation was far less favorable. In 1874 Lieutenant Colonel George A. Custer had led an expedition of gold-hungry miners into the Black Hills. The miners soon moved into Sioux hunting grounds and demanded protection from the US Army. Although Custer's detachment was annihilated in 1876 at the Battle of the Little Bighorn, the following year Congress redrew the lines of the Fort Laramie Treaty, seized the Black Hills, and forced the Sioux onto permanent reservations. The legal battle for ownership of the Black Hills continues to the present day.[10]

Apache (1954) further underscored the government's assimilation policies that explicitly demanded a loss of Indian identity. The movie begins with Geronimo's surrender in 1886 and tells the story of Massai (Burt Lancaster), known as the last Apache warrior. In the movie the US government forcibly removes the Chiricahua to a Florida prison, but Massai escapes by jumping off the train and flees to the New Mexico Territory. The warrior dismisses any compromise with white civilization and deplores the thought of living on a reservation. A Cherokee's plea for reconciliation because "we found that we could live with the white man, only if we lived like him" sends Massai scurrying off into the remote desert.[11]

Like a fugitive on the loose, Massai leaves a trail of murder and destruction as he flees the shackles of frontier law. Taunted by local citizens, pursued by a mob, and even bitten by a dog, the Indian is described as having "nothing in him but hate."[12] But love tames a wild soul, and when Massai "settles down" with an Indian woman, the cries of his newborn child prompt him to toss his rifle aside and call off the war. "He has planted corn," says one soldier, "something no other Apache has done before."[13]

But historically Massai never took up farming and instead lived a life hunting, foraging, and raiding as an outlaw in the southwestern desert.

He was reportedly killed in an ambush in 1911.[14] United Artists, however, wanted a more peaceful finale so they transformed Massai into a decent hard-working farmer.[15] *Apache* thus advocates the government's policy during President Grant's administration of implementing farming to integrate Indians into American society.

Jim Thorpe—All American (1951) was one of Hollywood's first postwar attempts to show a modern Indian hero within contemporary society. As a biographic representation of the great Olympic athlete, the Warner Bros. drama featured Burt Lancaster in the lead role and hired Thorpe as the movie's technical advisor then announced that the former athlete "did not want to cover up shadowy phases of his career."[16] Instead of creating a bleak story, producer Everett Freeman preferred to highlight the postwar concepts of tolerance and brotherhood. The movie's message, he believed, should "help promote better understanding between white men and their Indian brothers." Freeman's solution was to soften the movie's tragic Indian theme and instead stress "a tribute to a great athlete."[17] The studio thus attempted to reconcile Thorpe's feats on the gridiron, track, and baseball fields with the loss of his Olympic gold medals, the death of his infant son, and his rapid decline into oblivion.

James Francis "Jim" Thorpe was born in 1887 to an Irish/Sac-Fox father and a part French and Potawatomi/Kickapoo mother in what was formerly Indian Territory in Oklahoma. He attended the Carlisle Indian School where he plunged into sports and met the famed football coach Glenn S. "Pop" Warner. In 1912 Thorpe won two gold medals for the pentathlon and decathlon events at the International Olympics in Stockholm, Sweden, but the medals were revoked in 1913 when the Amateur Athletic Union accused him of playing professional baseball.[18] For the remainder of his life, Thorpe eked a meager living as a minor player in Hollywood movies while campaigning against studios hiring non-Indian actors for Indian roles.

Aware of Thorpe's various misfortunes and mishaps, Warner executives vacillated over whether to portray him as a victim or a hero. "The theme which occurs to me relies on the fact that Jim Thorpe is an Indian," Warner screenwriter and producer Milton Sperling wrote early in production, possibly influenced by the new trend in Native-based stories.[19] But the idea of a world-famous athlete—Indian or not—confined to life's dumps proved unattractive, so the studio opted for a more uplifting conclusion.

Jim Thorpe—All American thus resolves Thorpe's dilemma by making him an American hero. Thorpe says he just wants a chance to prove himself but discovers that the road to racial equality is long and arduous. He's passed over as football coach because he's Indian, and the Olympic committee demands return of his two gold medals. Thorpe believes that people want him back on the reservation: Following his son's death and marital break-up, he entertains in a carnival sideshow. But the movie eventually returns Thorpe to Oklahoma and appoints him an honored coach of a boy's football team. His dignity restored, Thorpe emerges as the Native American hero who has survived the battle scars of social bigotry and thus successfully adjusted to white American society.

The movie's optimistic conclusion, however, glossed over the former athlete's later years. Thorpe drifted in and out of movies playing only bit roles and took odd jobs as a laborer. Sadly, a reporter discovered the great athlete digging ditches for a mere $4 a day. Thorpe later sold the rights of his story *The Red Son of Carlisle* to Metro-Goldwyn-Mayer (with Clark Gable in the lead), but the picture was never made.[20] "He was doing a lot of drinking, and there was no money coming in," his daughter Grace

Thorpe explained.[21] Thorpe's death two years later of a heart attack at his trailer home was a far cry from Hollywood's optimistic ending.[22]

The loss of Indian identity gradually became the unavoidable price of assimilation. Many fifties Westerns thus offered a strong plea for racial assimilation in which Natives would be at the very least coerced to adopt the lifestyle and customs of white society. Universal's *Walk the Proud Land* (1956) takes place during the era of Grant's Peace Policy when Christianity and farming became the solution to hostile Indian/white relations. The movie recounts the story of agent John Clum (a youthful Audie Murphy) and his adventures on an Apache Indian reservation. The struggle between the US military and the Interior Department comes to a head when Clum tells the Army to stop exterminating the Indians and instead make useful citizens out of them. Clum's goal is to assimilate Indians into white culture—by force if necessary. He tells an Apache boy that he should learn white man's ways because "it's his world and you must learn to live in it" and asks Geronimo (Jay Silverheels) and his warriors to surrender and put themselves "under the mercy of the U.S. government."[23]

Clum forces the Apache to remain within the boundaries of the reservation and embrace white civilization. He sees himself as "a friend of the Indians" and tells the Army to return the pride and dignity that the military initially took away from them. Clum even requests that the Apache form their own police force modelled after the US military and offers them rifles. And in a special ceremony that recalls the mingling of the blood of two different racial groups in *Broken Arrow*'s wedding sequence, Clum and an Apache are joined together as blood brothers.

Another postwar film, *Navajo* (1952), attempted to introduce Native customs and beliefs but could not escape Hollywood's postwar agenda of forced assimilation. As a feature-length dramatization through the eyes of

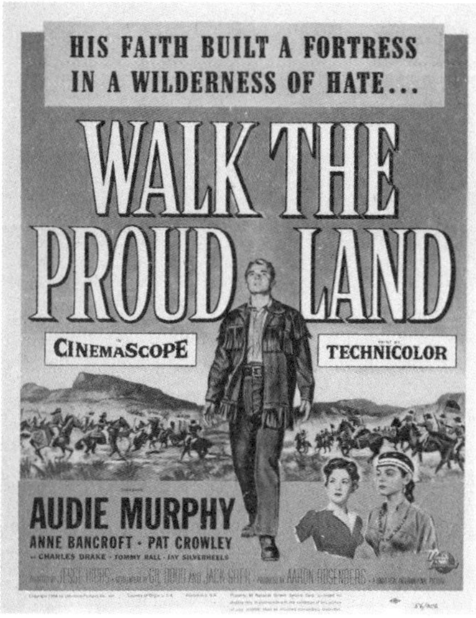

Figure 4.2. Poster for *Walk the Proud Land.* Courtesy of Walmart.

a seven-year-old Navajo boy, the movie was a far cry from the Indian "docudramas" of the 1930s like *The Silent Enemy* (1930) and *Eskimo* (1933) that had championed Native lifestyle over white civilization. *Navajo* instead proposed that Indians can be led to eventually abandon their traditional ways.

Filmed during the postwar era of Federal Termination, *Navajo* appeared to endorse the government's policies of assimilation. Independent producer Hall Bartlett joined with writer/director Norman Foster and hired mostly Navajo in the picture including the young Francis Kee Teller.[24] The black-and-white film was shot on location on the Navajo Reservation near Chinle, Arizona, and revolves around a rebellious lad (Teller) who distrusts all whites and vows never to join them. The boy escapes the stifling conditions of a local boarding school with his kindly white teacher (portrayed by producer Bartlett) and a Ute scout trailing him through remote canyons. Instructor and guide become injured, but the boy eventually realizes that not all white folks are evil. The final scene of the young lad running for assistance suggests that understanding and compassion will convince even the most rebellious Indian to join white society. The Protestant Motion Picture Council agreed and proudly presented *Navajo* with an award of exceptional merit.[25]

Other Westerns not only advocated postwar assimilation but offered Christianity as a solution to Indian/white conflicts. *Pillars of the Sky* (1956) opens in 1869 on a peaceful Oregon reservation where the missionary physician (Ward Bond) has converted many tribal members and baptized them with biblical names. (The title refers to the scenic Wallowa Mountains and their alpine peaks in northeastern Oregon.) Although a sympathetic sergeant (Jeff Chandler) tries to keep peace, the Army plans to open a road through the reservation and build a fort. The Yakama chief Kamiakin (Michael Ansara) refuses any peace deal with whites and sneers that his tribe will not be "swallowed up in the belly of a different people."[26] His alliance of Native leaders retaliates and declares war, capturing two white women and killing many troopers.

Assimilation, in the form of Christianity, brings peace to the warring community. The missionary pleads with Kamiakin for the survivors' safety, but the chief instead kills him. Another Indian leader, deeply ashamed of the chief's cowardly actions, kills Kamiakin and thus eliminates the rebellious warrior. In the movie's final scenes, the remorseful chiefs ask the sergeant to take the place of the missionary, and together Indians and whites kneel to listen attentively while the sergeant reads from the Bible.

Historically, Kamiakin fled to British Columbia then settled in the

Territory of Washington. *Pillars of the Sky* again shows the consequences when "good" Indians accept Christianity and "bad" Indians (like Kamiakin) do not.

While about half of the postwar Westerns promoted a kind of interracial brotherhood, several portrayed Natives in a less-than-favorable light. Paramount's postwar Westerns, for example, relied upon the Indian-as-obstacle formula in stark contrast to the sympathetic Native characters of Twentieth Century-Fox, Universal, and Warner Bros. Earlier Paramount Westerns like *The Plainsman* (1936), *Unconquered* (1947), and *Geronimo* (1939) had shown that any kind of Indian/white brotherhood was but a dream among the politically liberal. In fact, Paramount was often criticized for being "too conservative in its artistic policies" and rarely explored controversial topics of race relations under the leadership of its head of production Y. Frank Freeman (1938–1959).[27]

Paramount's *Arrowhead* (1953) intentionally mocked *Broken Arrow*'s ideals of a postwar brotherhood, and its pessimistic tone anticipated *The Searchers* by three years. *Arrowhead* appears as a reactionary response to the liberal bent of well-meaning films at the time and suggests that the rampant slaughter of innocent lives on the frontier will cease only when one race exterminates the other. The movie exposes the ugly prejudice on America's frontiers where both Indian and white protagonists have a fanatic hatred toward the other race. Bannon (Charlton Heston) is an Army scout with a long-standing grudge against the Apache for the murder of his parents; Toriano (Jack Palance) is an educated Apache, a "murderous and treacherous chief who leads his people in a bloody rebellion against the U.S. Cavalry" according to Paramount's publicity. A studio ad warns that although Toriano may be dressed in a jacket and tie, "under these gentlemanly garments beat a savage heart."[28]

Figure 4.3. *Arrowhead* mocked *Broken Arrow*'s ideals of postwar brotherhood. Courtesy of IMDb.

Arrowhead quickly dismisses *Broken Arrow*'s friendly policies toward Apaches as a fantasy. A naïve officer preaches peace and trusts the promises of the chief, but he is slain by Apaches. Bannon, on the other hand, believes that "the only good Apache is a dead Apache" and that treachery will result from making peace with Indians.[29] One scene flips *Broken Arrow*'s message of interracial harmony: Bannon sneaks upon Toriano, slashes his wrist, and forces his Apache enemy to become a blood brother. The movie's anti-Apache theme did not escape critics. "Whatever feelings of friendship for the American Indian may have been shown in a few open-minded Hollywood Westerns lately," observed the *New York Times*, "it is plain that producer Nat Holt is having no truck with any such ideas."[30]

Television's postwar Westerns, however, became popular at the same time on the small screen and preferred stories of noble Indian heroes. The earliest TV Westerns primarily targeted children and advocated peace and compromise on the frontier. But by the mid-1950s the genre was becoming tremendously popular to all ages as Western series jumped from only one in 1949 to twenty-three in 1955.[31] Enthusiastic fans, meanwhile, began to call for more pro-Indian dramas. "The public loves the Indian stuff," announced producer Sam Marx, adding that Cochise would therefore show up more heavily in TV's version of *Broken Arrow* (1956–1958), and that all future scripts of the series would focus on Indian life and lore.[32] The audience was apparently pleased: ABC's *Broken Arrow* scored 25.4 million viewers in its weekly half-hour time slot, ahead of both CBS and NBC. In fact, *Broken Arrow* was one of three TV programs (along with *I Love Lucy* and *Disneyland*) that parents allowed their children to stay up later to view.[33]

Broken Arrow featured the fair-haired boyish John Lupton as Jeffords who had also played the hero in the CBS pilot by the same name.[34] Several months later ABC picked up the series and aired 72 episodes beginning September 25, 1956. Syrian-born actor Michael Ansara portrayed Cochise, a role that turned him into a star. But privately, Ansara was frustrated by the character's limitations. "Cochise could do one of two things," he said. "Stand with his arms folded, looking noble; or stand with his arms at his sides, looking noble."[35] Ansara did admit, however, that playing the stoic chief actually helped his career. "I've never had so many offers and most are for non-Indian roles," he boasted.[36]

The TV series essentially followed the same storyline of the movie *Broken Arrow*. Jeffords strikes a friendship with Cochise and reprimands the rebellious Geronimo (Michael Pate) for agitating Apache warriors.

Figure 4.4. Michael Ansara as Cochise in TV's *Broken Arrow*. Author's collection.

Again, he falls in love with Sonseeahray, and again, she is killed. Elliott Arnold was delighted with the series because his acclaimed novel *Blood Brother* served as the source, and he was named story supervisor and editor. "It is the present policy of the sponsors that we have more action in the stories and that we work in Indians in every segment," Arnold lectured his writers.[37]

Like its movie predecessor, TV's *Broken Arrow* emphasized a pro-liberal agenda and promoted tolerance between Apaches and whites. The series also showed the Apache perspective of the Old West, which included indictments against greedy settlers, foolish government agents, and ignorant military officials along with accusations of the Army's genocidal policies. But while the film had opened with Jeffords's narrative point of view, the television series initially introduced each episode with Cochise and Jeffords as "equals." The early opening sequences of *Broken Arrow* intercut both characters approaching the other on horseback from opposite directions, with Cochise riding from the right and Jeffords on the left. The distinctive ridges and tilted formations of the Vasquez Rocks (northern Los Angeles County) provide a picturesque backdrop as the two men meet in the middle ground then grasp each other's forearms against the western sky.

Like Daves's original film, TV's *Broken Arrow* reinforces that good Indians follow white peace plans while bad Indians do not. Cochise, a friend to the whites, personally eliminates the bad Indians often led by Geronimo, who refuses to stay on the reservation and prefers to raid homesteads. "Geronimo insults me by raiding so close to my land," Cochise complains when the renegade warrior and his party attack a wagon and kill a man.[38] The dichotomy between good and bad Indians is clear, and Jeffords convinces Cochise to trust the US government to mete out justice rather than rely upon vengeful warriors.

The episode "Return from the Shadows" (1956) reinforces the theme of white justice. The segment yet again creates the story of Lieutenant George Bascom whose false accusations against Cochise had prompted the Army to unjustly hang the Apache chief's relatives. In this fictitious version of the Bascom Affair, the Army officer (renamed George Haskell) actually returns to Chiricahua territory to atone for the tragic event that triggered years of Apache/white warfare. The Apache want to kill Haskell, but Jeffords says that white law and not Apache revenge must dominate. He instead orders Haskell to return to the Army to face punishment.[39]

Similarly, the judge in "Apache Massacre" (1957) upholds law and order when a rancher retaliates against one of Geronimo's attacks by burning down an Apache village, killing innocent women and children. But the court restores justice when an all-white jury actually votes to hang the white culprit. Another *Broken Arrow* episode, "The Duel" (1958), even offers a lasting Apache/white union when a shopkeeper from the east romances a Chiricahua girl. Jeffords suffers from flashbacks of his doomed relationship with Sonseeahray, but the shopkeeper is undeterred and chooses to marry the girl.

Occasionally, these Indian/white friendships became "safe" metaphorical stand-ins for Black/white relationships. Television of the postwar era featured a few series with Black performers with variety shows like *Amanda* (1948–1949), *Stairway to Stardom* (1950–1951), and *The Hazel Scott Show* (1950) along with comedies *Beulah* (1950–1953) and *The Amos 'n Andy Show* (CBS, 1951–1953). But executives feared that controversial stories of race relations and civil rights could prompt boycotts among Southern viewers, causing writers to instead turn to "safer" parables that cast other minorities as victims.[40] "So instead of a Negro," one scholar explained, "[the writer] gives battle against that prejudice visited on American Indians or Alaskan Eskimos or Armenian peasants under the Czar."[41]

A year before *Broken Arrow* CBS launched *Brave Eagle* (1955–1956), produced by Roy Rogers Frontier Productions with Keith Larsen in the title role as the fictional Cheyenne leader. *Brave Eagle* gave youngsters a lesson in racial understanding and highlighted prejudice through ignorance. "In this program the Indians are the heroes, outwitting the stupid—and wicked white men," noted the weekly trade magazine *Broadcasting Telecasting*.[42] Like Cochise, Brave Eagle worked with the US Army to help keep peace and capture renegade Indians who resisted Anglo-American law and order. (The series was initially named *Cochise*.[43]) *Brave Eagle* also incorporated *Broken Arrow*'s theme that there are good Indians and bad Indians, just as there are good and bad white men.[44]

Brave Eagle featured the first Native American woman in a leading television role. Kim Winona was born Constance Elaine Mackey (1930–1978), and both her parents were from the Santee Sioux (Dakota) Nation in Nebraska.[45] Unfortunately, her character seldom delved beyond her romantic interest in the often-shirtless Larsen. Additionally, Hopi child actor Anthony Numkena (b. 1942) played Kenna in *Brave Eagle* and had previously portrayed the Indian boy adopted by Tyrone Power in *Pony Soldier* (1952).[46]

TV's postwar Westerns continued the tradition of noble Indian characters, cultured and educated by white institutions, well into the 1960s. Sam Buckhart (Michael Ansara) of NBC's *Law of the Plainsman* (1959–1960) was an educated Apache with a law degree from Harvard University. He saved the life of a US Cavalry officer after an Indian ambush, and when an officer died he left Buckhart money to attend Harvard. Buckhart then returns to the southwest and maintains law and order as Deputy US Marshal.[47] The opening scene establishes Buckhart's heroic stature as he sits proudly atop his white horse and gallops across the western horizon. Another highly educated Indian was Mingo (Ed Ames) of NBC's *Daniel Boone* (1964–1970). The loyal Mingo was the son of a Cherokee mother and an English father and was Oxford educated.[48]

Television's sympathetic Native American characters eventually evolved into heroes of contemporary stories. One of them appeared in ABC's *The Untouchables* (1959–1963) starring Robert Stack as Eliot Ness with syndicated columnist and radio commentator Walter Winchell as narrator. This gritty and violent crime series in which Ness fought Al Capone's gang featured Mexican-American actor Abel Fernandez as Prohibition Agent William Youngfellow, a Cherokee from Oklahoma. Youngfellow was actually inspired by real-life Agent William Jennings Gardner

(1884–1965), a Chippewa from North Dakota's Turtle Mountain Reservation who had attended Carlisle.[49]

From *Broken Arrow*'s many successors to TV's Westerns, the noble warrior motif had transformed Indian/white relations on the screen. Daves's movie, however, also prompted cautious stories of interracial romantic relationships. Although *Broken Arrow*'s Indian/white romance ended tragically, subsequent Westerns showed that these mixed relationships could survive. The white man might pair with an attractive Indian maiden like Cyd Charisse in *The Wild North* (1952), Debra Paget in *White Feather* (1955), or Elsa Martinelli as the Sioux chief's daughter in *The Indian Fighter* (1955), but in these movies the couples actually enjoy a lasting union.

Other Westerns occasionally reversed the cliché of a white man/Native woman romance. *Foxfire* (1955) showed the marital woes of an Apache mining engineer (Jeff Chandler) and a privileged white woman (Jane Russell). The two made an odd couple with Chandler's docile manner versus Russell's rather truculent behavior as she stomped through the town's dirt roads in her high heels. Despite their trials and tribulations, they somehow remained together. In *Hondo* (1953) John Wayne uncharacteristically plays an Apache (revealed in the film's early dialogue) who later marries a white woman (a miscast Geraldine Page). Likewise, in *Reprisal!* (1956), a Native man (Guy Madison) must fight the town's prejudice to prove his innocence for a murder he did not commit. He ultimately leaves the bigoted community with his Caucasian bride-to-be.[50]

Regardless of the many postwar interracial romances in films it inspired, *Broken Arrow*'s own tragic Indian/white marriage still raises objections. Writers have criticized the character of Sonseeahray as reinforcing the sacrificial "Indian Princess" or Pocahontas stereotype. After all, the camera often frames her as a "child of nature" among white birch trees

Figure 4.5. *Foxfire* shows a marriage between an Apache mining engineer (Jeff Chandler) and a privileged white woman (Jane Russell). Author's collection.

or a quiet river with a picturesque backdrop of red rocks. Sonseeahray appears soft, gentle, and physically attractive with honey skin and long flowing black hair. With her childlike innocence, she is fascinated with civilization, especially when Jeffords shows her his mirror and explains how she can see herself. She later muses, "The world is so big, and I know so little."[51] Likewise, *Broken Arrow* shows that when Sonseeahray is killed Jeffords tenderly holds her bullet-wounded body in his arms. For some, that visual symbol makes the movie's portrayal of her death even more dramatic and reminiscent of the Pocahontas legend.[52]

But unlike Pocahontas, who aids the white man and is forced to abandon her own culture, Sonseeahray remains closely tied to her Apache heritage. Her presence in the film is instead a narrative device that provides an opportunity for Jeffords to enter her world and learn Chiricahua customs. Jeffords is indeed naïve outside his own culture: His clumsy attempts to shoot a straight arrow prompt Sonseeahray to laugh and say, "I can do better myself!" Cochise is amused and retorts, "Never mind. By the time he is a grown man, he will know how."[53] Through his brief marriage to Sonseeahray Jeffords temporarily "goes Indian" and quicky discovers what is acceptable and what is not.[54]

Many writers have blamed the Production Code of 1934 and its anti-miscegenation clause as the apparent reason for Sonseeahray's death. But the Code itself was not hostile to Indian/white marriages and therefore did not force *Broken Arrow* to punish Sonseeahray and Jeffords.[55] Sonseeahray's romance with a white man actually fell within the Code's boundaries because its definition of miscegenation prohibited relations only between the Black and white races. According to the Code (part 2, item 6), "miscegenation (sex relationships between the white and black races)" was forbidden with no mention of miscegenation between whites and any race other than Black Americans.[56] In fact, mixed-race couples remained together in almost half (forty-five percent) of seventy-seven movies depicting miscegenation from 1946 to 1959.[57] Files from the Production Code Administration for *Broken Arrow* show no documentation that its authorities objected to the Jeffords/Sonseeahray romance, which closely followed Arnold's depiction in *Blood Brother*.

Lasting romantic unions between Natives and whites on film did occur long before *Broken Arrow*. Earlier movies had explored these mixed marriages, predominantly between white males and Native women. *The*

Bronze Bride (1917), *The Heart of Wetona* (1919), and *Behold My Wife!* (1934) all featured lasting Indian/white unions. Even DeMille departed from his tragic Indian/white relationship in *The Squaw Man* (1914) in which the Native woman marries a white man, but when her husband sends their son to England for a "proper" education she tragically kills herself. Conversely, in *The Woman God Forgot* (1917), DeMille shows that the captain of Cortez's army falls in love with and remains with an Aztec woman.

Nevertheless, the Production Code's anti-miscegenation clause has caused much confusion. Hollywood trade newspapers, for example, failed to grasp the nuances of the Code's anti-miscegenation clause and its relationship to white America. Some writers extrapolated the clause to mean that any mixed racial romance was forbidden while others attempted to clarify that the Code applied to only Black/white relations.[58] In MGM's *Across the Wide Missouri* (1951) a white fur trapper (Clark Gable) marries a Blackfoot woman (Mexican actress María Elena Marqués) and has a son. But the happy union tragically ends when angry warriors kill her. "A Blackfoot arrow, guided by the Production Code's anti-miscegenation line, cut down Gable's bride," *Time* magazine nonchalantly concluded in its review. The error frustrated MGM publicist Robert M.W. Vogel, who suggested that the studio should respond to the critics' frequent snipes at the Code so that they "at least, stop making mistakes."[59]

Other interracial relationships—or at least the suggestion of them—included Asian/white unions in *Japanese War Bride* (1952), *The Purple Plain* (1954), and *House of Bamboo* (1955). Mexican/white unions also occurred in films ranging from the low-budget noir Western *The Lawless* (1950) to the Warner Bros. epic drama *Giant* (1956). *Conquest of Cochise* (1953) proposes a last-minute Mexican/white union as a kind of antidote to Apache/white tensions when a Mexican landowner's daughter (Joy Page) falls in love with Cochise (John Hodiak). But the Apache leader refuses to let her live the life of a renegade, so she instead departs with the handsome Army officer (Robert Stack).

The murky issue of mixed racial relations has led many writers to conflate the movies' Indian/white romances as standing in for Black/white unions. Historically, American attitudes toward Indian/white marriages have been distinctly different from those of Black/white, which were once viewed as a form of "racial contamination." American policymakers, on the other hand, had encouraged Indian/white marriages as a means for Native people to leave their tribe and merge with the white race. In other words, these unions had been used as an assimilation tool to encourage the *disappearance* of Native tribes.[60] Whether intentional or not, many postwar Westerns also appeared to promote Indian/white unions as another form of forced assimilation in which Natives would eventually abandon their culture and adapt to white society.

From the country's vast frontiers to its urban centers, postwar Westerns and TV series had ventured into new territory by suggesting a commonality between Natives and whites. But *Broken Arrow*'s ideal of mutual coexistence demanded a sacrifice of Native identity, and Daves's version of a peaceful Indian/white co-existence began to reveal practical and political fissures. Hollywood's Native Americans would not escape being victims of racism and bigotry and would face years of alienation on the Western frontier.

Epilogue

The success of *Broken Arrow* opened the door to more opportunities for its cast and crew. Delmer Daves continued to direct, write, and produce for another fifteen years until he retired. His last period Western was *The Hanging Tree* (1959), and his final film was *The Battle of the Villa Fiorita* (1965). He was awarded a star on the Hollywood Walk of Fame on February 8, 1960, but never received an Oscar nomination for his vast body of work. He died in 1977.

Elliott Arnold continued to publish many books and wrote for TV Westerns like *Broken Arrow, Bonanza,* and *Rawhide.* He was married to actress Glynis Johns (the suffragette mother in *Mary Poppins*) and died in New York City in 1980.

After his refusal to answer questions in front of HUAC in 1947, screenwriter Albert Maltz was cited for contempt of Congress, sent to federal prison, and blacklisted by Hollywood. He later fled to Mexico and wrote under a pseudonym. Maltz was finally employed again on *Two Mules for Sister Sara* (1970), which was a vehicle for the popular actors Clint Eastwood and Shirley MacLaine. He died in 1985.

Michael Blankfort, who served as a front for Maltz on *Broken Arrow,* continued writing screenplays and novels in Hollywood. He was president of the Writers Guild of America, West, from 1967 to 1969, and he served on the Academy's Board of Governors from 1969 to 1971. He died in 1982.

Broken Arrow established Jeff Chandler as a star. He later signed a contract with Universal and performed as a singer in Las Vegas. He created his own company, Earlmar Productions, and starred in its Western, *Drango* (1957), about a post–Civil War Union Army officer. "It's no Indian story," Chandler said of the film. "Let Cochise rest in peace."[1] Chandler later formed another company, August Productions, for Allied Artists. He died tragically following disk herniation surgery at the age of forty-two.

The diminutive Debra Paget also gained stardom from *Broken Arrow* and signed a long-term contract with Fox. She appeared in Paramount's massive epic *The Ten Commandments* (1956) as Lilia, the Hebrew slave who served as a "water girl," then starred opposite Elvis Presley in *Love Me Tender* (1956). Her final two films, *Tales of Terror* (1963) and *The Haunted Palace* (1963), were for Roger Corman's American International Pictures. Paget was briefly married to director Budd Boetticher in 1960 then later retired from the screen.

Jay Silverheels, who played Geronimo, continued with his costarring role as Tonto in ABC's *The Lone Ranger* (1949–1957). When the series ended, he struggled to escape his TV image and appeared in guest roles in many Western series. Meanwhile, he worked diligently behind the scenes to support Native American actors and founded the Indian Actors Workshop in the late 1960s, where he encouraged Natives to develop their talent and compete for roles. He appeared with his students in Disney's *Smith!* (1969), in which the group received credit as the Indian Actors Workshop of Hollywood. Later, four Native Americans from the workshop landed roles in *Little Big Man* (1970).[2] In 1979, the Hollywood Chamber of Commerce honored Silverheels with a star on the Hollywood Walk of Fame.[3] He suffered a stroke, and in 1981 he died from complications of pneumonia.

While the majority of *Broken Arrow*'s cast and crew enjoyed successful Hollywood careers, the movie's concluding message of a postwar brotherhood was a far cry from the tragic outcome for the Chiricahua Apache. The film's narration suggests that the peace won by Cochise and Jeffords remained permanent. But in 1876, two years after Cochise's death, President Grant abolished the Chiricahua Reservation in southeastern Arizona and relocated the Chiricahua north to the San Carlos Apache Reservation.

Cochise's eldest son, Taza, became chief of the Chiricahua, but he died in 1876. Naiche, the younger son of the great Chiricahua Apache chief, inherited the leadership, and in the 1880s, he joined Geronimo and his warriors and bolted the reservation to raid in the United States and Mexico and fight against military campaigns. During the summer of 1886, the Apache surrendered at Skeleton Canyon in southern Arizona.

The worst atrocities were yet to come. Geronimo and about thirty-four followers, including women and children, were herded onto railroad cars and sent to Florida prisons. They were the first of five groups of Chiricahua confined in Florida out of a total of 515 Apaches. The military divided the families, sending the men to Fort Pickens in Pensacola and their wives and children to Fort Marion in St. Augustine. Two years later, the military moved the Chiricahua to the Mount Vernon Arsenal in Alabama. The families were finally reunited, but stifling humidity and malaria plagued the Apache prisoners. Their children, forced to abandon their culture and traditions, were sent to Carlisle boarding school, where approximately one quarter of the original 112 Apache students died.[4]

In 1894, the Chiricahua were once again removed to an Army base in

Figure 5.1. Cochise historical marker, Dragoon Mountains. Author's collection.

Fort Sill, Oklahoma, where they remained as prisoners of war until 1913. Upon release, many were relocated to Mescalero, New Mexico, and the remaining were resettled on small allotments scattered in southwestern Oklahoma. Today, numerous Chiricahua live on the Mescalero Apache Reservation in New Mexico and among the Fort Sill Apache Tribe in Oklahoma.

Naiche, Cochise's younger son, was forced to abandon much of his own culture and adopt the language, attire, and religion of white society. He joined the Dutch Reformed Church and was given a new Anglo name, Christian Naiche. He cut his hair and wore the uniforms of an infantry scout at Mount Vernon and a cavalry scout at Fort Sill. Naiche was a successful cattleman but struggled with bouts of alcoholism.[5] Still, he became a notable artist by painting depictions of Chiricahua culture like the maidenhood ceremony.[6] He lived his final years in Mescalero with the last of his remaining three wives and five of his fourteen children. Naiche died of influenza in 1919.[7]

In 1934, the Progressive Pioneers Club of the Cochise County Historical and Archeological Society and the US Forest Service erected a marker honoring Naiche's father. The plaque refers to Cochise as the "greatest of Apache warriors" and greets visitors at the entrance to the Cochise Stronghold Campground in the Dragoon Mountains.

Somewhere within those sharp canyon crevices lies the remains of Cochise, who died in 1874. Those few who knew the exact location of his burial in the Dragoons took the secret to their graves.

NOTES

INTRODUCTION

1. Scholars of Native American studies have different opinions about the plural form for members of nations, some preferring the collective form, as in Apache, some using the plural form with a terminal *-s*, as in Apaches. I have chosen to use the plural *-s* form throughout when describing scenes of specific movies or historical events or for consistency with other treatments in context.

2. See Angela Aleiss, "Hollywood Addresses Postwar Assimilation: Indian/White Attitudes in *Broken Arrow*," *American Indian Culture and Research Journal* 11, no. 1 (1987): 67–79. Much has changed since the publication of my article. For instance, back then, it was not widely known that Michael Blankfort had served as a front for the movie's blacklisted screenwriter Albert Maltz.

3. A few Native actors did play supporting or minor roles: Jay Silverheels (Canadian Mohawk) portrayed Geronimo, William Wilkerson (Cherokee) played Juan, Charles Soldani (Osage) was Skinyea, Robert Foster Dover (Navajo) played Machogee, Chris Willow Bird (San Ildefonso Pueblo) was Nochalo, and John War Eagle (Yankton Sioux) was Nahilzay. See chapter 2.

4. Richard Slotkin, *Gunfighter Nation: The Myth of the Frontier in Twentieth-Century America* (University of Oklahoma Press, 1998), 726n36. Slotkin had interviewed Daves during a symposium on Western movies in Sun Valley, Idaho, on July 2, 1976.

5. *Fort Apache*, "Notes on Cochise," box 5, folder 8, John Ford Manuscripts, Lilly Library, Indiana University, Bloomington.

6. Several writers have argued that Daves's film and subsequent Westerns paralleled the Black experience in America. See John H. Lenihan, *Showdown: Confronting Modern America in the Western Film* (University of Illinois Press, 1980); Edward Buscombe, *"Injuns!": Native Americans in the Movies* (Reaktion Books, 2006), especially chapter 2, "The Liberal Western," 101–50; and Steve Neale, "Vanishing Americans: Racial and Ethnic Issues in the Interpretation and Context of Post-war 'Pro-Indian' Westerns," in *Back in the Saddle Again: New Essays on the Western*, edited by Edward Buscombe and Roberta Pearson (British Film Institute, 1998), 8–28.

7. The guild's vote for posthumous recognition was reported in the *Los Angeles Times* on June 29, 1991, F1, and July 3, 1991, SDF2. Its formal presentation of the award to Maltz was reported in the *Los Angeles Times* on March 24, 1992, F2, and March 25, 1992, VYB12. In 1997, the Writers Guild restored Maltz's credit as screenwriter for *The Robe* (1953); see *New York Times*, April 3, 1997.

8. *Los Angeles Times*, June 29, 1991, F1. Although I use the popularized name and acronym for this body (House Un-American Activities Committee, HUAC), the official name was the House Committee on Un-American Activities (HCUA).

9. See, for example, Jacquelyn Kilpatrick, *Celluloid Indians: Native Americans and Film* (University of Nebraska Press, 1999); Jeff Smith, *Film Criticism, the Cold War, and the Blacklist: Reading the Hollywood Reds* (University of California Press, 2014); and Stanley Corkin, *Cowboys as Cold Warriors: The Western and U.S. History* (Temple University Press, 2004). Corkin argued that *Broken Arrow* raises doubt about its idealized conception of Apache autonomy and actualities of reservation life which he describes as "anything but a kind of Gulag in which poverty, alcoholism, and cultural isolation proliferate" (110). Reservations were part of government-to-government agreements between Native Americans and the United States. In my opinion, the comparison to Gulags reinforces negative perceptions of Native peoples and ignores the special trust relationship between Native nations and their land.

10. See Glenn Frankel, *High Noon: The Hollywood Blacklist and the Making of an American Classic* (Bloomsbury USA, 2017), xiii.

11. Frank Manchel, "Cultural Confusion: *Broken Arrow* (1950)," in *Hollywood's Indian: The Portrayal of the Native American in Film*, edited by Peter C. Rollins and John E. O'Connor (University Press of Kentucky, 1998), 91–106. If movies have a responsibility to accurately reflect history, the problem then becomes that "experts"—scholarly or otherwise—often disagree over what is really accurate.

12. Andrew Patrick Nelson, "Don't Be Too Quick to Dismiss Them: Authorship and the Westerns of Delmer Dave," in *ReFocus: The Films of Delmer Daves*, edited by Matthew Carter and Andrew Patrick Nelson (Edinburgh University Press, 2016), 57.

CHAPTER 1

1. *Los Angeles Herald-Examiner*, June 2, 1985, F4. See also Elizabeth Pelletier Jones, "Letters from the Blacklist: The Un-Friendship of Albert Maltz and Michael Blankfort" (MA thesis, Boston University, 2017), 22.

2. Elliott Arnold, "Problems in Adapting Novel to Movie Related by Author," *Arizona Daily Star*, August 16, 1950.

3. Arnold, "Problems in Adapting."

4. Arnold said that he based his story on writings between Jeffords and Arizona historians as well as anthropologists and ethnologists. He also relied on notes from the Arizona Pioneers' Historical Society and the University of Arizona Library. See Elliott Arnold, *Blood Brother* (Duell, Sloan and Pearce, 1947), author's note.

5. In 1854, the United States acquired from Mexico the region in present-day southern Arizona and southwestern New Mexico through the Treaty of Mesilla. The event is often referred to as the Gadsden Purchase.

6. Numerous books have told the story of Cochise and the Chiricahua. Three by Edwin R. Sweeney are among the most authoritative accounts: *Cochise: Chiricahua Apache Chief* (University of Oklahoma Press, 1991); *Making Peace with Cochise: The 1872 Journal of Captain Joseph Alton Sladen* (University of Oklahoma Press, 1997); and *Cochise: Firsthand Accounts of the Chiricahua Apache Chief* (University of Oklahoma Press, 2014). See also Dan L. Thrapp, *The Conquest of Apacheria* (University of Oklahoma Press, 1975).

7. Several writers have erroneously referred to the book's title as *Blood Brothers* (plural). The title is *Blood Brother* (singular), which begs the question: To whom does blood brother refer?

8. Arnold, *Blood Brother*, author's note.

9. Arnold's author's note in *Blood Brother* states that Jeffords confided to close friends that he was "intimate with a lovely Indian girl," although none of his biographers have corroborated that assertion. Others say Jeffords was "a lifelong, dedicated bachelor"; see C. L. Sonnichsen, "Who Was Tom Jeffords," *The Journal of Arizona History* 23, no. 4 (Winter, 1982): 384. Doug Hocking has written an entire book on Jeffords; see *Tom Jeffords: Friend of Cochise* (TwoDot, 2017).

10. Jeffords was not the first white to approach Cochise about a peace agreement. Sweeney noted that in late 1868, the Apache chief sent a message to Colonel Thomas Devin that he would agree to end hostilities in return for a reservation in southeastern Arizona. Devin, however, did not have the means that were available years later to General Howard. Additionally, Cochise gave several interviews from 1870–1871, and in 1872, Colonel Gordon Granger had even invited the Apache chief to Washington, DC, but Cochise refused. See Sweeney, *Cochise: Firsthand Accounts of the Chiricahua Apache Chief*, 123–24, 187–92.

11. Arnold, *Blood Brother*, 3.

12. Sweeney, *Cochise: Firsthand Accounts of the Chiricahua Apache Chief*, 30n4.

13. *Los Angeles Times*, November 25, 1956, F1. Jeffords had actually met Cochise before he and Howard ventured to the Dragoons in October 1872; see Sweeney, *Cochise: Firsthand Accounts of the Chiricahua Apache Chief*, 202–3n23, and Hocking, *Tom Jeffords: Friend of Cochise*, 99–101.

14. Certificate of the Bronze Star Medal to Elliott Arnold, 21 April 1950, series 7, box 15, folder 16, Papers of Elliott Arnold, 1920–1980, courtesy of the University of Arizona Libraries Special Collections, Tucson.

15. *New York Times*, May 14, 1980, B6.

16. See Helen Emmons, Original Certificate of Birth, 6 March 1919, Arizona State Board of Health, Bureau of Vital Statistics, and Miss Helen

Emmons to Elliott Arnold, marriage August 6, 1943, *Newspapers.com Marriage Index, 1800s to current*, Ancestry.com.

17. Most likely, Helen had read the story "War Chief," by Hal Mitchell, in the May 1945 edition of *Arizona Highways*.

18. *Los Angeles Times*, November 25, 1956, F1.

19. *Tucson Daily Citizen*, February 23, 1950, 9.

20. Larry Ceplair, "Julian Blaustein: An Unusual Movie Producer in Cold War Hollywood," *Film History*, 21, no. 3 (2009): 260.

21. *Los Angeles Times*, May 21, 1950, D1. *Blood Brother* was turned down by several studios because of extensive costs involving location shooting and transport of cast and crew. Burt Lancaster and Harold Hecht's Norma Productions had initially purchased the rights to Arnold's novel; see *New York Times*, September 8, 1948, 38.

22. "Recollections of Nunnally Johnson," interviewed by Tom Stemple, *An Oral History of the Motion Picture in America*, 31, the Regents of the University of California, 1969.

23. *Los Angeles Daily News*, October 17, 1949.

24. Ceplair, "Julian Blaustein," 260.

25. Barbara Zheutlin and David Talbot, "Albert Maltz: Portrait of a Hollywood Dissident," *Cinéaste* 8, no. 3 (1978): 9.

26. Ronald Reagan and Albert Maltz, Testimony before HUAC, 1947, US Congress, House, Committee on Un-American Activities, Hearings (1947).

27. *Variety*, April 12, 1950, 2.

28. *The Screen Writer*, June–July 1948, 12.

29. *New York Times*, May 8, 1949, BR:5.

30. *Variety*, April 13, 1949, 7, and April 20, 1949, 14.

31. Blacklisted writers Howard Lawson and Dalton Trumbo filed an appeal on behalf of the Ten to overturn their contempt citations. The US Supreme Court refused to hear their appeal on August 1949. Beginning in mid-summer 1950, Maltz would serve ten months in federal prison working as a medical orderly; *Los Angeles Times*, April 28, 1985.

32. *UPI.com* (website for *United Press International*), 15 July 1982.

33. *Los Angeles Times*, June 29, 1991, F1, and *Los Angeles Herald-Examiner*,

June 2, 1985, F1. The *Los Angeles Times* had reprinted the August 21, 1948, letter from Blankfort to Maltz. Jones mentions that only Maltz, Blankfort, and Blaustein knew of the arrangement; see Jones, "Letters from the Blacklist," 25.

34. *Los Angeles Times*, June 29, 1991, F16.

35. Albert Maltz, "What Shall We Ask of Writers?," *New Masses*, February 12, 1946, 19. The article brought strong attacks from fellow party members, and Maltz was forced to write a retraction two months later; see Maltz, "Moving Forward," *New Masses*, April 9, 1946, 8. By the mid-1950s, Maltz had severed all relations with the Communist Party. In 1957, the party published an article forgiving Maltz for his initial stance on art and politics; see Larry Ceplair and Steven Englund, *The Inquisition in Hollywood: Politics in the Film Community, 1930–1960* (University of California Press, 1983), 236, 474.

36. Zheutlin and Talbot, "Albert Maltz," 5.

37. Albert Maltz, "Author's Foreword" to *Blood Brother: A Screenplay Based upon the Novel by Elliot [sic] Arnold*, December 10, 1948, box 10, Albert Maltz Collection #150, Howard Gotlieb Archival Research Center, Boston University [Albert Maltz Collection].

38. Maltz, "Author's Foreword" to *Blood Brother*. Maltz had written that the story's events occurred from 1870 to 1872.

39. See Maltz, *Blood Brother: A Screenplay Based upon the Novel by Elliot [sic] Arnold*, passim.

40. In his screenplay version, Maltz instead used a complex internal monologue: Jeffords walks away from the crowd and fumes over the community's racism while simultaneously rebuking himself for falling in love with an Apache girl. See *Blood Brother*, 86.

41. *Arrow* (tentative title for *Broken Arrow*), "Conference on Revised Final Script of 11 June 1949," June 13, 1949, 1–2, Cinematic Arts Library, University of Southern California.

42. See John Belton, *American Cinema/American Culture* (McGraw-Hill Higher Education, 2022), 297. In private correspondence, Belton explained that the lynching scene actually combines *both* political and racial issues. Lynching

as a subject has appeared in 273 Westerns since the early silent films, according to the *AFI Catalog*. Earlier movies like *Fury* (1936) and *They Won't Forget* (1937) also contain a disturbing lynching scene but are non-Westerns.

43. The entire "Bascom affair" appears in *Blood Brother* in chapter 7 of the first book, where Arnold specifically deals with the fatal meeting between Cochise and Bascom. A later film, *The Battle at Apache Pass* (1952), focuses on this incident and its tragic consequences (see chapter 4).

44. Blaustein actually had proposed a historical conclusion in which Bascom has a conference with Cochise, Jeffords, and Howard over the kidnaped boy and threatens the Apache leader. Cochise escapes, but Sonseeahray is shot and killed. Howard promises to court-martial Bascom, and Jeffords becomes Apache agent of the reservation. Blaustein, step-by-step scenario #2, n.d., 11–12, Julian Blaustein, series 3, box 3, folder "Script File: 1948–1949, *Blood Brother*," Albert Maltz Collection, American Heritage Center, University of Wyoming.

45. See Sweeney, *Making Peace with Cochise* for Sladen's account of his journey with General Howard to locate Cochise. Sladen was also a physician.

46. *Arrow*, "Conference with Mr. Zanuck (on Final Script of May 20, 1949)," June 1, 1949, 3–4, Cinematic Arts Library, USC. Arnold, in fact, initially included brief stories of Jeffords's two additional love interests in the first draft of his novel; see *Blood Brother*, first draft, 1949, 98, 278–81; series 3, box 2, Papers of Elliott Arnold. The characters of both Terry and Sonseeahray also appeared in his draft.

47. Maltz, *Blood Brother*, 89; and Daves, *Broken Arrow*.

48. See Arnold, *Blood Brother*, 25–27, 55–57.

49. Delmer Daves, *Broken Arrow*, 1950. In Maltz's script, *Blood Brother*, 126–29, Geronimo breaks from Cochise's band at the end of the story.

50. George Elwood Jones, "The American Indian in the American Novel, 1875–1950" (PhD diss, New York University, 1958), 520, 523. See also Jeanne C. Herbert, "The Growth of Realism in the Treatment of the Southwestern Indian in Fiction since 1900" (MA Thesis, University of Arizona, 1961), 49.

51. Arnold, *Blood Brother*, 3.

52. Arnold, *Blood Brother*, 24.

53. *Broken Arrow*, incomplete draft, 1949, 111, series 3, box 3, folder 3, Papers of Elliott Arnold.

54. Arnold, *Blood Brother*, 144–45. Many Apache refer to the Bascom affair as "cut the tent" or "cut through the tent," describing Cochise's cutting a hole in the tent to escape after Bascom threatened to hold him as a hostage.

55. Arnold, *Blood Brother*, 176–79, 85–86. Sweeney mentioned that while Apache cruelty was often prompted by white and Mexican violence, some of their victims were infants and children whose mutilated bodies were savagely beaten. See Sweeney, *Cochise: Firsthand Accounts of the Chiricahua Apache Chief*, 64, 84n13.

56. Arnold, *Blood Brother*, 436–37; 450. The red blanket was reportedly a gift from Henry C. Hooker (1828–1907), owner of the Sierra Bonita Ranch near Willcox, Arizona, one of the oldest cattle ranches in the United States. See Sweeney, *Cochise: Chiricahua Apache Chief*, 396–97; and Hocking, *Tom Jeffords*, 187n22. Although Arnold wrote that the name Cochise was woven into the blanket, others say that only a capital C appeared in its center; see Hocking, 118.

57. Maltz, *Blood Brother*, 34, 37.

58. John Belton, *American Cinema/American Culture* (McGraw-Hill Higher Education, 1994): 218.

59. *New York Times*, July 21, 1950, 15.

60. Daves, *Broken Arrow.*

61. Daves, *Broken Arrow*. A wikiup is a kind of circular hut made from interlaced branches or brushwood. The dwelling is intended to be temporary in nature.

62. Daves, *Broken Arrow.*

63. Maltz, *Blood Brother*, 116–18; and Daves, *Broken Arrow*. According to Sweeney in *Cochise: Chiricahua Apache Chief*, Nahilzay was killed by neither Jeffords nor the Chiricahua chief. Nahilzay first joined Cochise's son Taza when the Chiricahua moved to San Carlos Reservation in 1976 then bolted with Naiche in 1881 and was later captured and sent to a prison in Chihuahua, Mexico (459n72).

64. Maltz, *Blood Brother*, 319–21.

65. Maltz, *Blood Brother*, 77A–79.

66. To me, the movie's visual reference to the 1876 Battle of the Little Bighorn is obvious. During that battle, George Armstrong Custer held the rank of lieutenant colonel.

67. The sudden and surprise attack on the wagon train was a typical strategy. Apache warriors, however, preferred to initiate their attacks and ambushes by foot and to use their horses to move quickly across the battlefield before dismounting and fighting. Warriors would often target the horses in the opening seconds of their ambush, which would cripple their enemies' ability to pursue. See Robert N. Watt, "Raiders of the Lost Ark: Apache War and Society," *Small Wars and Insurgencies* 13, no. 3 (Autumn 2002): 12. Watt wrote that the historic parallel to the wagon train attack in *Broken Arrow* was the Lakota/Cheyenne/Arapaho ambush of Captain William J. Fetterman in 1866. Watt, email to author, May 10, 2022.

68. Maltz, *Blood Brother*, 30A.

69. "Conference with Mr. Zanuck (on Final Script of 20 May 1949)," June 1, 1949, 1–2, Cinematic Arts Library, USC.

70. "Conference with Mr. Zanuck (on Final Script of 20 May 1949)," June 1, 1949, 2, Cinematic Arts Library, USC; and Daves, *Broken Arrow*.

71. In *Blood Brother*, Arnold first mentions the "blood brother" ceremony between Cochise and Mangas Coloradas on page 19. Interestingly, no blood brother ceremony existed in Arnold's early draft of his novel. *Blood Brother* first draft, second part (no date), series 3, box 2, Papers of Elliott Arnold.

72. Arnold, *Blood Brother*, 368–69; and Jones, "'The American Indian in the American Novel, 1875–1950," 315–16. The drinking (as opposed to sucking) of blood recalls the vampire legend, although I can find no reference to that specific ritual in literature.

73. See, for example, Jeffords's obituaries in the *Tucson Citizen*, February, 20, 1914, 8, and *Arizona Daily Star*, February 20, 1914, 1.

74. Brent Buckner, former cultural coordinator, Fort Sill Apache Cultural Program, Oklahoma, interview by the author, March 16, 2022.

75. Morris E. Opler, *An Apache Life-Way: The Economic, Social, and Religious Institutions of the Chiricahua Indians* (University of Chicago Press, 1941),

162; and Eve Ball, *Indeh, An Apache Odyssey* (Brigham Young University Press, 1980), 31. Ball noted that the novel *Blood Brother* is valuable for historical and anthropological authenticity except for a few details.

76. Daves, *Broken Arrow*.

77. See James L. Haley, *Apaches: A History and Culture Portrait* (Doubleday & Company, 1981), 144. Haley has no mention of a formal wedding ceremony, although he referred to the custom of both man and woman temporarily living alone following their marriage.

78. See Arnold, *Blood Brother*, 359–65, 452.

79. Arnold, *Blood Brother*, 453. Shortly before his death, Cochise told Jeffords that he hoped they would meet again someday "up there, I think, beyond that hill" (449).

80. Larry Ceplair, "Who Wrote What? A Tale of a Blacklisted Screenwriter and His Front," *Cinéaste* 18, no. 2 (1991): 19.

81. *Arrow*, Temporary Script, April 11, 1949, Delmer Daves Papers (M192), Department of Special Collections, Stanford University Libraries (hereafter Delmer Daves Papers).

82. *Arrow*, Final Script, May 20, 1949, and Revised Final Script, June 11, 1949, Delmer Daves Papers.

83. In *Making Movies Black: The Hollywood Message Movie from World War II to the Civil Rights Era* (Oxford University Press, 1993), the late historian Thomas Cripps wrote that all the dead in *Broken Arrow* are Indians, "as though a warning that entering white circles can only result in death" (281). Both Chip and Ben Slade are in fact killed by the Apache.

84. Daves, *Broken Arrow*.

85. See Jon Cowans, *Empire Films and the Crisis of Colonialism, 1946–1959* (Johns Hopkins University Press, 2015), 258. Cowans argued that Sonseeahray's death is key to the movie's peace agreement.

86. Daves, *Broken Arrow*.

87. After an agreement between Cochise and General Howard to set aside land for the Chiricahua, President Grant created the Chiricahua Indian Reservation by executive order in 1872. See US Grant, "Chiricahua Reserve,"

Executive Mansion, December 14, 1872, 4, in *Executive Orders Relating to Indian Reserves,* May 14, 1855, to July 1, 1902, compiled by the Indian Office under Authority of Act of Congress, approved May 17, 1882.

88. Daves, *Broken Arrow.*

89. Ceplair, "Who Wrote What?," 19. Ceplair also noted that *The Robe* (1953) was initially credited to Philip Dunne, but in 1997, the opening credits were altered to include Maltz; see Ceplair, *The Marxist and the Movies: A Biography of Paul Jarrico* (University Press of Kentucky, 2007), 241.

90. Zheutlin and Talbot, "Albert Maltz," 15.

91. *New York Times,* April 29, 1985, D10. *The Execution of Private Slovik* was eventually made as an NBC-TV movie in 1974. Maltz intended to sue Sinatra for $75,000 but settled for half the amount; see Jones, "Letters from the Blacklist," 115.

92. Zheutlin and Talbot, "Albert Maltz,"14.

93. *Los Angeles Herald-Examiner,* June 2, 1985, F4. See also Jones, "Letters from the Blacklist," 25.

94. Ceplair, "Who Wrote What?," 21.

95. See *Los Angeles Herald-Examiner,* June 2, 1985, F4; and Maltz to Blankfort, March 23, 1964, in Jones, "Letters from the Blacklist," 122.

96. *Los Angeles Times,* June 29, 1991, F16.

97. Blankfort to Blaustein, November 18, 1980, in Jones, "Letters from the Blacklist," 266.

98. Blankfort to Maltz, October 13, 1980, in Jones, "Letters from the Blacklist," 266.

99. Notes by Dorothy Blankfort on letter from Blaustein, March 24, 1984, in Jones, "Letters from the Blacklist," 276.

100. *Los Angeles Times,* June 29, 1991, F16.

CHAPTER 2

1. Don Tollefson, "Delmer Daves on Film: Past, Present, and Future," *The Stanford Daily,* 2 March 1972, 6.

2. Tollefson, "Delmer Daves on Film," 6.

3. Delmer's father, Arthur, was head of the family and a wholesaler in a millinery. Arthur's wife, Nannia P., was born in Utah, and her mother came from Ohio; see Thirteenth Census of the United States, Ocean Park City, Ballona, California, April 30, 1910, Ancestry.com.

4. Oral History Program at Columbia University: Popular Arts Project, Interview with Delmer Daves by Mr. and Mrs. Robert C. Franklin, series 3, vol. 7, no. 322, June 1959, 31.

5. Both Louis A. Daves (ca. 1859–1882) and George Daves (1867–1888) appear to be the brothers of Daves's grandfather. Louis is buried in Tombstone's legendary Boothill Graveyard in Cochise County. George is buried in the "new" Tombstone Cemetery, just to the west of Boothill. See entries for Louis Austin Daves and George Daves on Ancestry.com.

6. Christopher Wicking, "Interview with Delmer Daves," *Screen: The Journal of the Society for Education in Film and Television* 10, no. 4–5 (1969): 59.

7. A few writers have said that Daves received his law degree at Stanford, but his son Michael explained that Delmer only studied law and never pursued a graduate degree; Michael Daves, interview by author, June 4, 2022. Delmer entered Stanford as an undergraduate in 1922; as a member of the class of 1926, he remained at Stanford for an extra year before leaving. *Stanford Daily*, May 10, 1927, 1, and September 5, 1929, 4.

8. *Stanford Daily*, December 10, 1923, 1.

9. *Stanford Daily*, July 23, 1926, 1, and January 4, 1926, 2; *The Stanford Quad* (Stanford yearbook), Class of 1926, 110, 289, 337, and 273.

10. Oral History Program at Columbia University, 32.

11. Oral History Program at Columbia University, 32–33.

12. Oral History Program at Columbia University, 4. The "1914 film" was likely *Christmas Memories* (1915), a Universal movie starring Robert Z. Leonard and Ella Hall. Daves recalled that both actors were in the film.

13. Al Horowitz, Director of Publicity, Columbia Studios, Biography of Delmer Daves, Margaret Herrick Library, Academy of Motion Picture Arts and Sciences (hereafter, AMPAS). *The Duke Steps Out* is believed to be a lost film.

14. Oral History Program at Columbia University, 4, 7; and Wicking, "Interview with Delmer Daves," 55, 56.

15. Bertrand Tavernier, "The Ethical Romantic," *Film Comment* 39, no. 1 (Jan/Feb 2003): 46.

16. Nelson, "Don't Be Too Quick to Dismiss Them," 29.

17. *Silver Screen*, January 1936, 71.

18. *Los Angeles Times*, June 12, 1938, B1; and Delmer Lawrence Daves and Mary Lou Lender, Marriage License, State of California, County of Los Angeles, County Marriages 1850–1952, 11 July 1938, FamilySearch.org.

19. *Los Angeles Times*, September 28, 1991, A30.

20. *Beverly Hills Citizen*, February 9, 1960, 3; *Los Angeles Herald Examiner*, May 9, 1963, F7; and *Hollywood Diary*, June 15, 1961.

21. Nelson, "Don't Be Too Quick to Dismiss Them," 30; and Tavernier, "The Ethical Romantic," 46–47. Although Delmer had registered for the Selective Service in World War II, he did not serve in the military; Michael Daves interview, June 4, 2022.

22. Daves, *Hollywood Canteen* (1944). The Golden Gate Quartet had a nationwide radio program and the opportunity to sing at FDR's inauguration in 1941.

23. Michael Daves, interview by author, July 16, 2022. Delmer Daves was initially scheduled to direct *Johnny Belinda* (1948), but Warner Bros. instead chose Jean Negulesco; *Hollywood Reporter*, December 5, 1946, 1.

24. Michael Daves, interview by author, June 16, 2022, and July 16, 2022.

25. Michael Daves, June 16, 2022, interview. IMDb lists seventy-one credits for Michael, although four are uncredited.

26. Michael Daves, June 16, 2022, interview.

27. *Variety*, February 9, 1949, 7.

28. *Exhibitor*, February 21, 1951, SS-3.

29. *Variety*, February 9, 1949, 7; *Motion Picture Daily*, February 24, 1949, 3; and *New York Times*, April 13, 1949, 39.

30. Blaustein, Letter to Daniel Taradash (screenwriter), April 10, 1949, Daniel Taradash Papers, AMPAS. Blaustein favored Daves for director but was disappointed that Nicholas Ray was not available.

31. Michael Daves, July 16, 2022, interview.

32. Oral History Program at Columbia University, 31.

33. Oral History Program at Columbia University, 33.

34. Delmer Daves, Letter to Thomas Cripps, March 2, 1971. Cripps was an emeritus professor of history at Morgan State University in Baltimore.

35. Daves, *Broken Arrow.*

36. *Los Angeles Times,* May 21, 1950, D1.

37. Wicking, "Interview with Delmer Daves," 65–66; and Tavernier, "The Ethical Romantic," 44. For close-ups or reaction shots, Daves would typically film on sound stages; see *Dallas Texas Catholic,* November 3, 1956, 13. For me, many of the close-ups in *Broken Arrow* look like they were shot in the studio.

38. Daves, *Broken Arrow.*

39. Blaustein to Harry O. Parks (Secretary, Willcox Chamber of Commerce), April 6, 1949, AHC. The Willcox Chamber of Commerce is located about thirty miles from the nearby Cochise Stronghold.

40. Writers occasionally confuse the Chiricahua National Monument as the location of the Cochise Stronghold where Jeffords and General Howard met the Apache chief. The Cochise Stronghold lies within the Dragoon Mountains in the Coronado National Forest, part of the US Forest Service (Department of Agriculture). The Chiricahua National Monument is part of the US National Park Service (Department of the Interior), which lies about forty-six miles to the southeast of the Dragoons.

41. China Camp is believed to be eight miles west of Stronghold Canyon. Sweeney notes that Captain Sladen described the area and "the gate" at the entrance; see *Making Peace with Cochise,* 148n83; and Hocking, *Tom Jeffords,* 185n33.

42. The name Dragoon Mountains comes from the Dragoon Pass at its north end, through which the US Army's Dragoon regiment manned many military posts in the late 1850s. With the Gadsden Purchase of 1854, the Dragoons and surrounding area became part of the United States. The mountains were previously referred to as the Sierra de la Peñascosa, or a very rugged, rocky range.

43. *Arizona Daily Star,* October 22, 1948, B1; and *Coconino Sun,* May 27, 1949, 1. An extra, a term once used in the industry to refer to someone who performs in a nonspeaking role in the background, is now commonly referred to as a background actor.

44. Oral History Program at Columbia University, 33.

45. Todd McCarthy, "John Ford and Monument Valley," *American Film* 3, no. 7 (May 1978): 16.

46. Joseph Taft, ed. "Dialogues with a Director," *Persimmon Hill* 5, no. 2 (1975): 44. *3:10 to Yuma* had only a brief scene shot in Sedona.

47. Tavernier, "The Ethical Romantic," 42, 44.

48. "Preliminary Location Survey," *Arrow*—Story #305, April 25, 1949, Delmer Daves Papers, and *Los Angeles Times*, May 21, 1950, D1. The movie's working title was *Arrow*; see *Motion Picture Daily*, February 24, 1949, 3. The title was later temporarily changed to *War Paint*; *Variety*, July 20, 1949, 16.

49. Clarence D. Hutson, "Location Survey for the *Arrow* Production," Report to Mr. Ray A. Klune, May 16, 1949, 4–5, Delmer Daves Papers. Hutson, manager of the studio's location department, agreed that without the participation of Fort Apache's Tribal Council, it would have been risky to involve the tribe in the picture.

50. Taft, "Dialogues with a Director," 49.

51. Hutson, "Location Survey for the *Arrow* Production," 4–5; and Letter to Mr. Lester Oliver, Chairman, Tribunal Council, Whiteriver (Fort Apache) Agency, May 12, 1949, 1–3, Delmer Daves Papers. See also *Tucson Daily Citizen*, May 24, 1949, 16.

52. Hutson, Letter to Oliver, May 12, 1949, 1–3. A few scholars have pointed out that the studio agreed to pay white male drivers and riders a higher wage, at ten dollars per day for eight hours including lunch. Unlike the agreement with the Apache, however, the drivers' rate did not include lodging and three meals per day. Hutson, "Location Survey for the *Arrow* Production," 4–5. According to a SAG-AFTRA spokesperson, lodging and three meals per day would more than compensate for the difference in salary; interview by author, December 3, 2022.

53. Sadly, these Apache scouts were treated the same as the Chiricahua prisoners of war and shipped far from Arizona to Florida for incarceration (see epilogue).

54. Blaustein, Letter to A. E. Stover (San Carlos Indian Agency), October 21, 1948, Julian Blaustein, series 3, box 3, folder "Script File: 1948–1949, *Blood*

Brother," AHC. The ABC TV series *Broken Arrow* (1956–1958) would focus on the early reservation years (see chapter 4).

55. Brenda L. Haes, "The Incarceration of the Chiricahua Apaches, 1886–1914: A Portrait of Survival" (MS Thesis, Texas Tech University, 1997), 1–60 passim. After release, the Chiricahua divided into two groups, with the majority relocating to the Mescalero Apache Reservation in New Mexico and the remaining enrolled in the Fort Sill Apache Tribe of Oklahoma.

56. During an interview, Daves said that in addition to the White Mountain Apache, he had chosen eight Native Americans for speaking roles; see Heinz-Gerd Rasner et al., "Gespräche mit Delmer Daves," *Filmkritik* 19, no. 217 (January 1975): 31. Only six Natives actually appear in the movie's credits. Two additional actors, Iron Eyes Cody and his older brother J. (Joe) W. Cody, were not Native but Italian; see Angela Aleiss, "Native Son.," *Times-Picayune* (New Orleans), May 26, 1996.

57. For an in-depth discussion of Silverheels's heritage and his impact on Hollywood's Indians, see Angela Aleiss, *Hollywood's Native Americans: Stories of Identity and Resistance* (Praeger Publishers), 47–61.

58. Robert M. Dover's father was Filipino and his mother Navajo. See US Indian census rolls, 1885–1940, Northern Navajo Reservation, New Mexico (supplemental), January 1, 1938. According to the census, Dover was one-half Navajo.

59. John War Eagle, originally John Henry St. Pierre, was born in South Dakota. Numerous sources have confused him with another John War Eagle born 1902 in the United Kingdom. See *Rapid City Journal* (South Dakota), May 28, 1950, 20; St. Pierre, World War II Draft Registration Card, Serial No. 702; and US Indian census rolls, 1885–1940, Yankton Sioux Agency, South Dakota, June 30, 1913.

60. Willow Bird, World War II Draft Registration Card, Serial No. 2339, April 25, 1942; and US Indian census rolls, 1885–1940, northern Pueblo Agency, New Mexico, June 30 1922. Willow Bird's birth name was Hilario Pino, b. ca.1887.

61. See, for example, Charles L. Soldani on the US Indian census rolls, 1885–1940, Osage Reservation of the Oklahoma jurisdiction, April 1, 1933.

For Wilkerson, see *Sydney Daily Telegraph*, August 30, 1940, 3. Wilkerson also appears on the *Cherokee Nation, Cherokee Roll*, Card #520, May 21, 1906 (citizenship certificate issued May 15, 1907), and World War II draft registration card, ca. 1942.

62. *Saturday Review*, May 4, 1963; and Michael Daves, interview by author, July 16, 2022.

63. *Los Angeles Daily News*, December 20, 1948, 24. When I attended Delmer Daves's seminar in San Diego (see introduction), he humorously mentioned how he enjoyed working on close-ups with his leading women.

64. Michael Daves, July 16, 2022, interview.

65. Taft, "Dialogues with a Director," 46.

66. Niño Cochise, who claimed to be Cochise's grandson, said he had applied for the movie's lead Apache role and was turned down. See Ciyé "Niño" Cochise and A. Kinney Griffith, *The First Hundred Years of Niño Cochise* (Abelard-Schuman, 1971), 334–35. Many doubted Niño's claims that he was the son of Cochise's eldest son, Taza, who had died in Washington, DC, in 1876. Taza never had any children. In 1954, Niño was actually Robert Darwin Majors, convicted of writing bad checks and at that time told the press he was the grandson of Cochise; see *The Californian* (Salinas), July 31, 1954, 2.

67. See Sweeney, *Cochise: Chiricahua Apache Chief*, 262. No known photographs of Cochise exist, and several identified as the Apache leader are in fact misidentified. See Angela Aleiss, "Is This Really the Legendary Cochise?" *Indian Country Today*, October 12, 2016. I'm not sure why a few writers claimed that Chandler had blue eyes when his World War II draft registration card, issued October 16, 1940, under his real name, Ira Grossel (b. December 15, 1918), attested to their being brown; Ancestry.com.

68. Michael Daves, June 16, 2022, interview.

69. Taft, "Dialogues with a Director," 48.

70. Michael Daves, June 16, 2022, interview.

71. Taft, "Dialogues with a Director," 48. Following *Broken Arrow*, Chandler became a romantic icon to female audiences. But in 1999, his former girlfriend Esther Williams revealed in her book *The Million Dollar Mermaid* that he enjoyed cross-dressing because it "gave him a sexual thrill." The backlash was

swift; see *Los Angeles Times,* October 27, 1999, F2. One angry reader accused Williams of writing "the trashiest book of the decade"; see James Prideaux, Letter to the *Los Angeles Times,* October 30, 1999. But an LBGT youth outreach advocate responded, "Apparently it did not damage his acting ability or his virility. . . . Maybe those who are so upset now are afraid of their own little sexual proclivities being made public at some future time"; Virginia Uribe, Letter to the *Los Angeles Times,* October 30, 1999.

72. *Los Angeles Times,* July 30, 1950, D1.

73. *Saturday Review of Literature,* May 5, 1950, 31. The publication later changed its title to *Saturday Review.*

74. Wicking, "Interview with Delmer Daves," 63.

75. Opler, *An Apache Life-Way,* 123–24; and Haley, *Apaches,* 143. Opler also referred to the social dance custom as the "partner dance," an integral part of the girl's Puberty Rite.

76. See my discussion of the wedding ceremony in chapter 1. Screenwriter Maltz had lifted passages of the wedding from Arnold's novel, in which Arnold admits that he took a writer's liberty and imagined that such a wedding took place; see Arnold, "Author's Note," *Blood Brother.* See also Douglas Horlock, *The Films of Delmer Daves: Visions of Progress in Mid-Twentieth-Century America* (University Press of Mississippi, 2022), 121.

77. A few Grant biographers believe that his Peace Policy was rooted in destroying Native American culture in the fulfilment of Manifest Destiny. Robert E. Ficken has written that the Peace Policy essentially forced Indians to engage in farming, rather than hunting, and led to boarding schools; see "After the Treaties: Administering Pacific Northwest Indian Reservations," *Oregon Historical Quarterly* 106, no. 3 (2005): 442–61. Ron Chernow argued that although Grant favored mercy to Indians who abided by his policies, those who did not would have to be forced to submit to them; Chernow, *Grant* (Penguin Press, 2017), 659, 738. To his credit, Grant was the first president to appoint a Native American, Ely S. Parker (Seneca), as commissioner of Indian affairs. Parker resigned under pressure in 1871.

78. See Luana Ross, *Inventing the Savage: The Social Construction of Native American Criminality* (University of Texas Press, 1998), 4, 17. Ross shared the

belief with other scholars that federal assimilation policy during this time was more about colonization—the control over Native American people through economic inequity, racism, and loss of culture—rather than the adoption of the majority culture by an ethnic or racial group. For a more in-depth discussion, see Robert Blauner, "Colonized and Immigrant Minorities" in *From Different Shores: Perspectives on Race and Ethnicity in America*, edited by Ronald Takaki (Oxford University Press, 1987), 149–60.

79. John W. Ragsdale Jr., "The Chiricahua Apaches and the Assimilation Movement, 1865–1886: A Historical Examination," *American Indian Law Review* 3, no. 2 (2005/2006): 297–98, 308. Ragsdale argued that the Chiricahua Reservation was discussed from a position of balanced strength (313). But the tribe's confinement forced them to rely on government rations that not only disrupted their economic system but did not always arrive, resulting in widespread hunger and exposure during harsh winters. Jeffords, acting as tribal agent, was often exasperated. See Sweeney, *Cochise: Chiricahua Apache Chief*, 367–90 passim.

80. The movie's term *peace treaty* is misleading. Congress ended the practice of negotiating treaties with Indian tribes in 1871 and created reservations through executive order, thus placing new emphasis on legislation geared toward civilization and assimilation. The Indian Appropriation Act of 1871 made all Native Americans wards of the federal government, nullified all subsequent treaties with them, and provided that no Indian nation or tribe "shall be acknowledged or recognized as an independent nation, tribe or power with whom the United States may contract by treaty"; Indian Appropriation Act of 1871, 25 U.S.C. Sec. 71. See also Ragsdale, "The Chiricahua Apaches and the Assimilation Movement," 296.

81. Cochise addressed the raiding into Mexico in a tribal council meeting on November 21, 1873, and laid down the law: either his warriors refrain or leave the reservation. Both Juh and Geronimo refused to stop raiding and left. See Sweeney, *Cochise: Firsthand Accounts of the Chiricahua Apache Chief*, 275.

82. Daves, *Broken Arrow*. See Alicia Delgadillo and Mariam A. Perrett, eds. *From Fort Marion to Fort Sill: A Documentary History of the Chiricahua Apache Prisoners of War, 1886–1913* (University of Nebraska Press, 2013), xxiv. The editors

explain that the Apache would trade any surplus spoils acquired through raiding for items that they were unable to manufacture for themselves.

83. Daves, *Broken Arrow*.

84. A few scholars have suggested that *Broken Arrow* promotes multiculturalism instead of assimilation. Horlock said that Cochise agreed to peace primarily on his terms while surrendering nothing of his culture and way of life; see *The Films of Delmer Daves*, 116. Likewise, David N. Eldridge argued that "the [movie's] vision of Apache autonomy on a reservation seems closer [to] multiculturalism than to assimilationism, and it contradicts suggestions that the film aimed to support the current Termination Policy of closing the reservations and integrating Indians into American society"; see Eldridge, "Dear Owen,": The CIA, Luigi Luraschi, and Hollywood, 1953," *Historical Journal of Film, Radio and Television* 20, no. 2 (June 2000): 108–9. As discussed in chapter 3, Termination was another of the government's efforts to force Indians to abandon their culture and lifestyle and assimilate into white society.

85. Daves, *Broken Arrow*.

86. *Tucson Star Citizen*, July 9, 1950; July 5, 1950.

87. *Box Office Report*, "Top 15 Films of 1950 by Domestic Revenue," 1997–2005, boxofficereport.com

88. *Screen Directors Playhouse, Broken Arrow*, September 7, 1951. Previously, the story had been dramatized as a *Lux Radio Theatre* radio play on January 22, 1951, starring Burt Lancaster and Debra Paget.

89. The proposal was based on the case of Maria Hertogh (1937–2009), whose outcome brought about riots. See *New York Times*, December 13, 1950, 3; and *Los Angeles Times*, December 25, 1950, 2.

90. A film treatment is a brief summary of the story before the entire script is written.

91. Darryl Zanuck, inter-office correspondence to Casey Robinson, February 8, 1951, 1; and Robinson, inter-office correspondence to Zanuck, February 2, 1951, box 32, folder 1, page 3, Delmer Daves Papers.

92. Daves, inter-office correspondence to Robinson, April 11, 1951, box 32, folder 1, page 5; and Daves, "Early Western Version of Bali Story," no date, box 31, folder 9, Delmer Daves Papers.

93. "Biography of Delmer Daves," News Department, Warner Bros. Pictures, Inc., 1961, AMPAS.

94. *Technicolor News and Views*, December 1952, 2. Daves reportedly agreed under protest to take on the studio assignments of *Bird of Paradise* and *Treasure of the Golden Condor*; see *Films & Filming*, May 1, 1963, 48.

95. *New York Times*, October 19, 1941, X5.

96. Daves, inter-office correspondence to Zanuck, April 26, 1951, 4–5, box 33, folder 5, Delmer Daves Papers.

97. Zanuck, inter-office correspondence to Jules Buck [producer] and Joe Eisinger, January 19, 1951, 2, box 33, folder 7, Delmer Daves Papers.

98. Buck and Daves, inter-office correspondence to Zanuck, December 3, 1951, 1–2, box 33, folder 7, Delmer Daves Papers.

99. John H. Lenihan wrote that Daves presented the Indian's point of view in *Broken Arrow* and wanted to offer the settler's side of the story in *Drum Beat*; see *Showdown*, 43n12.

100. Daves, *Drum Beat*.

101. Syd Colombe, cultural preservation and education director of the Modoc Nation (Oklahoma), agreed that the movie's Modoc were not wearing their correct attire. Colombe, interview with author, January 4, 2023. See also *Arizona Daily Sun* (Flagstaff), May 18, 1954, 1.

102. Daves, *Drum Beat*.

103. Daves, *Drum Beat*. General Canby was the only US general ever killed in an Indian conflict. (George Armstrong Custer was a lieutenant colonel during the Battle of the Little Bighorn.) The Modoc War was such an embarrassment for Grant that he lost much of his enthusiasm for his Peace Policy. See Mary Stockwell, *Interrupted Odyssey: Ulysses S. Grant and the American Indians* (Southern Illinois University Press, 2018), 155.

104. Here I depart from the discussion of the film by Józef Jaskulski, "Bent, or Lifted Out by Its Roots: Daves' *Broken Arrow* and *Drum Beat* as Narratives of Conditional Sympathy," in *ReFocus: The Films of Delmer Daves*, 82–83; along with that of Horlock, *The Films of Delmer Daves*, 101–3.

105. Daves, *Drum Beat*. Notably, only Alan Ladd has a front credit as the star before the movie's title. The two females are relegated to co-starring roles.

106. For a brief summary of Toby Riddle's life, see Rebecca Bales, "Winema and the Modoc War: One Woman's Struggle for Peace," *Prologue Magazine* 37, no. 1 (Spring 2005). Bales cited Meacham's book, *Wi-ne-ma (The Woman-Chief) and Her People* (1876), as an excellent source.

107. Estimating Script, *Drum Beat*, April 9 1954, 102–14, and Final Script, May 17, 1954, 98–100, box 1863a, Warner Bros. Archives, USC Cinematic Arts Library.

108. Webb, *White Feather*.

109. *Citizen News* (Hollywood), December 13, 1954, 18.

110. Webb, *White Feather*. Paget was not the first choice for Appearing Day; She later replaced Rita Moreno who had a scheduling conflict. *Daily Variety*, June 22, 1954, 2, and *Variety*, August 11, 1954, 2.

111. See Horlock, *The Films of Delmer Daves*, 117. Horlock argued that Daves left the studio and that Tanner's closing narration does not represent the writer's intentions. Absent any further documentation, we really don't know what Daves's intentions were. But it's clear that for whatever reason, the studio revised the ending after the Final Draft Screenplay of July 1, 1954 (and the revisions to the Final Shooting Script of July 14, 1954). It is worth noting that "final" shooting scripts don't always match the actual release print.

112. On the Production Code's 1956 revisions, see *Motion Picture Daily*, December 12, 1956, 6–7; *Motion Picture Herald*, December 15, 1956, 13–15; and *New York Times*, December 16, 1956, X3.

113. *Daily Variety*, June 13, 1958, 3, and *New York Times*, December 15, 1957, 133. Other reviewers found the ending unsatisfactory; see *Motion Picture Daily*, June 13, 1958, 4. MGM's *The World, the Flesh and the Devil* (1959) starring Harry Belafonte also had shown an "inconclusive" Black/white union. The Production Code files for *Kings Go Forth* did not show any issues with the Wood/Sinatra relationship.

114. Daves, *Cowboy*. Borgnine and Jurado actually married in 1959.

115. Harry Brand, Director of Publicity, "Synopsis of *The Last Wagon*," 1956, 1, box 2, folder 1, Gwen Bagni Papers, 1940–2001, UCLA Special Collections, Gwen Bagni Papers.

116. Bagni, "*The Last Wagon*" (story and treatment), no date, box 2, folder 4,

109–10, 114–16, 22, 31, Gwen Bagni Papers. Bagni (1913–2001) was co-screenwriter for *The Last Wagon* and a television writer. William B. Hawks (younger brother to director Howard Hawks) produced *The Last Wagon*.

117. Daves, *The Last Wagon*. Susan Kohner, daughter of Mexican actress Lupita Tovar, was noted for portraying ethnic roles including a Mexican woman in *Trooper Hook* (1957) and the biracial daughter in *Imitation of Life* (1959).

118. In 1965, Daves worked on another "unrealized project," *Jackson Hole* for Warner Bros. The movie was his attempt to return to Westerns with his company Diamond D Productions. *Jackson Hole* was based upon the novel *The Honyocker* (1961) by Giles A. Lutz and was never filmed. But unlike the Bali/Western story that had only a treatment, *Jackson Hole* proceeded to a final script dated June 1, 1965. Daves had considered casting James Stacy in the lead; Michael Daves, interview, July 16, 2022.

119. Michael Daves, interview by author, June 16, 2022, and July 16, 2022.

120. *New York Times*, May 27, 1965, 28, and January 27, 2009, C3.

121. Michael Daves, interview, June 16, 2022.

122. *New York Times*, January 27, 2009, C3.

123. Daves, *Susan Slade*. If *only* Daves had shown more continuity in his career, but unfortunately, he just wasn't quite that kind of filmmaker.

124. The CBS television series *The Waltons* (1972–1981) was loosely based on *Spencer's Mountain*, also written by Earl Hamner Jr.

125. Lenihan, *Showdown*, 61.

CHAPTER 3

1. Clayton R. Koppes, "From New Deal to Termination: Liberalism and Indian Policy, 1933–1953," *Pacific Historical Review* 46, no. 4 (1977): 555–56; and Donald L. Fixico, *Termination and Relocation: Federal Indian Policy, 1945–1960* (University of New Mexico Press, 1986), 178. See also Larry J. Hasse, "Termination and Assimilation: Federal Indian Policy, 1943 to 1961" (PhD diss., Washington State University, 1974), 108, 110.

2. See Fixico, *Termination and Relocation*, xii, 77, 135, 145, 155, 157, 186; and Koppes, "From New Deal to Termination." The government later changed the name "relocation program" to "employment assistance." Many critics believed

that the program was really the government's way to get Indians off reservations and make their lands available to whites.

3. *Los Angeles Times*, February 23, 1989, A1; and *New York Times*, August 6, 1922, 5. On April 12, 1922, at his third and final trial, a jury acquitted Arbuckle of manslaughter. His reputation was nonetheless ruined. He found work behind the scenes, directing numerous short films. He died on June 29, 1933.

4. Twentieth Century-Fox Film Corporation, "*Broken Arrow* is Truly Great Movie," *Broken Arrow* Pressbook, New York Public Library at Lincoln Center (hereafter, *Broken Arrow* Pressbook).

5. "Magnitude, Theme Lend Importance to Coming Movie," *Broken Arrow* Pressbook.

6. "Type Lines—Did You Know?" and "Movie Shows Old Ceremony," *Broken Arrow* Pressbook.

7. "How to Solve Smoke Signals," "Small Town Exploitation Ads," and "Co-op Merchandising," *Broken Arrow* Pressbook.

8. *Motion Picture Daily*, July 10, 1950, 11; and *Variety*, June 12, 1950, 18.

9. "Actor Takes Own Chances," "Troubles Beset Screen Actress," "Actor Talks Up, Shut Up by Indian," and "Indians Deplore Whites' Lack of Medical Insight," *Broken Arrow* Pressbook.

10. Mary Beth Haralovich, "Motion Picture Advertising: Industrial and Social Forces and Effects, 1930–1948" (PhD diss., University of Wisconsin-Madison, 1984), 24–25, 32–33.

11. "Exhibitor's Campaign Book," *Broken Arrow* Pressbook.

12. Cecil B. DeMille, *Unconquered* (1947).

13. "Suggestions for Promotion of *Unconquered*," box 430, folder 7, pages 6, 10, Cecil B. DeMille Collections, Archives and Manuscripts, Harold B. Lee Library, Brigham Young University.

14. "Selling Ideas for *Unconquered*," *Unconquered* Pressbook, New York Public Library at Lincoln Center.

15. Suggested advertisements for newspaper features, *Broken Arrow* Pressbook.

16. *Variety*, June 28, 1950, 1, and September 27, 1950, 1.

17. Zanuck, Inter-Office Correspondence to Daves, June 15, 1950, box 29, folder 15, pages 1–2, Delmer Daves Papers.

18. Zanuck, Inter-Office Correspondence to Daves, June 16, 1950, 1, box 29, folder 15, Delmer Daves Papers.

19. *Tucson Star Citizen*, June 18, 1950.

20. *The New Republic*, July 31, 1950, 23; *The Rotarian*, November 1950, 36; *Newsweek*, August 7, 1950, 76; and *Christian Century*, September 13, 1950, 1087.

21. *Commonweal*, August 5, 1950, 413–14.

22. *New Yorker*, July 22, 1950, 63; and *Time*, July 31, 1950, 62.

23. *New York Times*, July 21, 1950, 15.

24. *Los Angeles Times*, August 19, 1950, 9.

25. *Daily Variety*, June 12, 1950, 3; *Independent Exhibitors Film Bulletin*, July 3, 1950, 8; *Harrison's Reports*, June 17, 1950, 94; and *The 20th Century Fox Dynamo*, April 1950, 45. *The Dynamo* was Fox's in-house promotional booklet.

26. Ellen C. Scott, "'We proudly present . . . the picture they didn't want you to see!': Black Film Advertisements, 1946–1960," *Black Camera* 5, no. 1 (Fall 2013), 23, 32.

27. *Los Angeles Sentinel*, July 20, 1950, B2; *Baltimore Afro-American*, July 29, 1950, 8; and *Chicago Defender*, July 8, 1950, 14. Portrayals of lasting romantic unions between Indians and whites had previously appeared in Hollywood films. See chapter 4.

28. Sherry Robinson, *Apache Voices: Their Stories of Survival as Told to Eve Ball* (University of New Mexico Press, 2000), 59. Published Native reactions to *Broken Arrow* at the time of the movie's release—other than a few studio promotional articles—were rare or even nonexistent. Black newspapers had been around since the late 1890s, but with the exception of the *Cherokee Phoenix* (which began in 1828), most Native American publications didn't really become prominent until the 1960s.

29. Naomi Hartford, interview by author, June 26, 2022.

30. Trudy Griffin-Pierce, *Chiricahua Apache Enduring Power: Naiche's Puberty Ceremony Paintings* (University of Alabama Press, 2006), prologue, 16.

31. Griffin-Pierce, *Chiricahua Apache Enduring Power*, 137, 148. The author noted that Sonseeahray was killed to satisfy the Production Code's disapproval

of miscegenation. The Code's anti-miscegenation clause did not extend to Indian/white relationships. See chapter 4.

32. In an article in *Arizona Highways* in August 1951, *Blood Brother*'s author, Elliott Arnold, credited the White Mountain Apache for their participation in the movie and based the Puberty Rite and masked Gahé dancers on Western Apache as opposed to Chiricahua culture. Arnold referred to the Puberty Rite as the ceremony of the big wickiup, or the coming out ceremony.

33. James Kunestsis, interview by author, July 22, 2022. Kunestsis, whose ancestors are Chiricahua, is a consultant with the Mescalero Apache Tribe Historic Office in New Mexico. He was also a leader of the Apache Crown Dancer Group, known as Gahé or Mountain Spirits; see *New York Times*, March 12, 2008, H32.

34. Kunestsis interview. The movie's Apache regalia was also problematic for Brent Buckner, former Cultural Coordinator of the Fort Sill Apache Cultural Program (see chapter 1, note 74).

35. *Long Beach Press Telegram*, June 25, 1949, 12. Stewart was single at the time but later married actress Gloria Hatrick McLean.

36. Liza Black, "Picturing Indians: American Indians in Movies, 1941–1960" (PhD diss., University of Washington, 1999), 266–67. See also Black's book on a similar subject, *Picturing Indians: Native Americans in Film, 1941–1960* (University of Nebraska Press, 2020).

37. Association of American Indian Affairs endorsement of *Broken Arrow*, released June 12 and distributed to newspaper syndicates, *Broken Arrow* Pressbook.

38. *Laughing Boy*'s financial loss is from the E. J. Mannix Ledger, "Loew's Inc. MGM Studios Operating Results by Pictures," AMPAS.

39. Oliver LaFarge, Letter to Miss Hormann, June 27, 1950, *Broken Arrow*, box 73, folder 6, 1949–1956, Association of American Indian Affairs, General and Tribal Files 1851–1983, Seeley G. Mudd Manuscript Library, Princeton University (hereafter, Association of American Indian Affairs).

40. "A Human Member of the Human Race," program for special preview screening for *Broken Arrow* at the Museum of Modern Art in New York City, July 13, 1950, 11–12, Association of American Indian Affairs.

41. "Remark of Vice President Edward G. Lindeman," Museum of Modern Art in New York City, July 13, 1950, 1–2, Association of American Indian Affairs.

42. See Harold Mantell, "Counteracting the Stereotype" (a report on the Association's National Film Committee), *American Indian* 5, no. 4 (Fall 1950), 16–17, 19.

43. "Remark of Vice President Edward G. Lindeman," 1–2.

44. Hasse, "Termination and Assimilation," 114.

45. La Farge, "Association of American Indian Affairs Restatement of Program and Policy in Indian Affairs," February 8, 1950, "Association on American Indian Affairs, 1950," Papers of Philleo Nash, Truman Library. Quoted in Hasse, "Termination and Assimilation," 114.

CHAPTER 4

1. *Hollywood Reporter*, February 22, 1955, 3.

2. *Motion Picture Daily*, September 8, 1954.

3. Cowans, *Empire Films and the Crisis of Colonialism*, appendix A, 347–48. Out of the fifty-one postwar Westerns, Cowans revealed that only fourteen featured anti-Indian portrayals while thirteen were mixed, or a combination of both positive and negative images.

4. For a new analysis of the "legend" surrounding the Bascom Affair, see Doug Hocking, *The Black Legend: George Bascom, Cochise, and the Start of the Apache Wars* (TwoDot, 2018). In *The Battle at Apache Pass*, the story's evil Indian agent Neil Baylor (Bruce Cowling), whose character was based on confederate officer John R. Baylor, dies at Apache Pass. In real life, Baylor lived until 1894 and was a Texas politician and first governor of the Arizona Territory, CSA.

5. Taza was Cochise's eldest son and succeeded his father when the chief died in 1874. He served as Chiricahua leader for only two years.

6. *New York Times*, November 26, 1954, 24.

7. In the movie, the white hero's Cherokee wife and infant son were killed in a massacre by soldiers. A bearded Rock Hudson, in an early supporting role, is Corporal Burt Hanna.

8. *New York Times*, February 19, 1951, 19.

9. George Sherman, *Tomahawk* (1951).

10. In *United States v. the Sioux Nation of Indians* (1980), the Supreme Court ruled that Congress had acted in bad faith when it broke the Fort Laramie Treaty. The court set compensation for the Black Hills at $102 million. The Sioux, however, refused this payment because they insist that the land is theirs by sovereign right.

11. Robert Altman, *Apache* (1954).

12. Altman, *Apache*.

13. Altman, *Apache*.

14. Other sources say that Massai died in 1906. See Sherry Robinson, "Massai and Zanagoliche: An Apache Abduction Turned Enduring Love Story," *Wild West* 25, no. 4 (December 2012): 22–23. According to the author, Massai was born in Arizona sometime in the 1850s and died in 1906.

15. Edwin T. Arnold and Eugene L. Miller, *The Films and Career of Robert Aldrich* (University of Tennessee Press, 1986), 24–25.

16. Production Notes on *Jim Thorpe—All American*, Warner Bros. Archives, USC Cinematic Arts Library.

17. Everett Freeman, to J. R. Nichols (Commissioner of Indian Affairs, 1949–1950), June 1, 1950, Warner Bros. Archives, USC Cinematic Arts Library. Freeman also shared screenwriting credit on the movie.

18. Robert W. Wheeler, *Jim Thorpe: World's Greatest Athlete* (University of Oklahoma Press, 1978), 110, 164.

19. Milton Sperling, Inter-office Correspondence to Freeman, December 1, 1949, box 1761, Warner Bros. Archives, USC Cinematic Arts Library.

20. *Motion Picture Herald*, January 9, 1932, 13. *The Red Son of Carlisle* was supposed to star Gable; *Hollywood Filmograph*, January 30, 1932, 4.

21. Interview with Grace Thorpe as quoted in Angela Aleiss, "Jim Thorpe: Olympic Athlete and Hollywood Frontrunner," *Indian Cinema Entertainment*, 1997/1998, 7.

22. *Los Angeles Times* (obituary), March 30, 1953, C1.

23. Jesse Hibbs, *Walk the Proud Land*, 1956.

24. *Los Angeles Times*, December 2, 1951, E4. Francis Kee Teller was born

in 1943 on the Navajo Reservation in Arizona. Both his father Lee Teller and mother Nattezbah appeared on the US Indian Census Rolls, 1885–1940, Southern Navajo Reservation, April 1, 1930, Arizona.

25. *New York Times*, February 11, 1951, 97; February 21, 1952, 24; and *Los Angeles Times*, July 11, 1952, B9.

26. George Marshall, *Pillars of the Sky*, 1956.

27. See the *New York Times*, May 18, 1959, 30; and January 29, 1950, 77. An exception was *The Lawless*, a 1950 movie about Mexican/white tensions in a California town. But *Time* noted that while it's a good movie, "considering its makers, it is also as unexpected as a slum documentary by Cecil B. DeMille"; *Time*, July 3, 1950, 76–78.

28. Publicity for *Arrowhead*, Paramount Press Sheets, 1952–1953, Paramount Collection, AMPAS.

29. *New York Times*, September 16, 1953, 38.

30. *New York Times*, September 16, 1953, 38.

31. Edward Buscombe, *The BFI Companion to the Western* (British Film Institute, 1988), 428.

32. *Variety*, October 31, 1956, 31.

33. *Broadcasting Telecasting*, February 18, 1957, 67; and *Television*, November 1957, 56.

34. An episode of the earlier *The 20th Century Fox Hour* anthology series had aired May 1, 1956, and featured Ricardo Montalban as Cochise. He was replaced by Michael Ansara for the TV series.

35. *New York Times* (obituary), August 3, 2013, B8.

36. *The Washington Post and Times Herald*, October 24, 1957, B11.

37. *Variety*, October 31, 1956, 35.

38. *Broken Arrow*, Season 1, Episode 13, "Apache Massacre," aired January 1, 1957.

39. Bascom died during the Civil War on February 21, 1862, in the New Mexico Territory.

40. *The Twilight Zone*'s writer and creator, Rod Serling, for example, was ordered to change a character inspired by Emmett Till, the fourteen-year-old Black victim of a brutal Mississippi lynching. The character instead became an

elderly Jewish pawnbroker to appease sponsors and executives for the "Noon on Doomsday" episode of *The United States Steel Hour* (CBS, 1956). See Lawrence Venuti, "Rod Serling: Television Censorship, *The Twilight Zone*," *Western Humanities Review* 35, no. 4 (Winter 1981): 355–57.

41. Venuti, "Rod Serling," 359. Venuti explained that advertisers ruled the airwaves during this era when a single brand would sponsor television programs, so executives were nervous about offending even a cereal manufacturer. See also *Variety*, October 2, 1957, 52.

42. *Broadcasting Telecasting*, October 17, 1955, 15, and *Motion Picture Daily*, October 3, 1955, 10.

43. *Ross Reports on Television*, May 25, 1955, 1.

44. *Motion Picture Daily*, October 3, 1955, 10.

45. Kim Winona's parents, Elaine Grace Garvie and Elmer Marion Mackey, were both listed on the US Indian Census Rolls as Santee Sioux. See US Indian Census Rolls, 1885–1940, Ponca and Santee and Yankton Sioux Indians, June 30,1918, Yankton Agency, South Dakota.

46. Numkena's father, Anthony (b. 1911), appeared on the US Indian Census Rolls, 1885–1940, Hopi Reservation, December 31, 1937, Arizona.

47. Ansara first played the same character of Sam Buckhart in TV's *The Rifleman* in the 1959 episodes "The Indian" and "The Raid" but neither served as a pilot for *Law of the Plainsman*.

48. Mingo was first introduced as Oxford educated in the *Daniel Boone* episode "Ken-Tuck-E" aired September 24, 1964 on NBC.

49. *Grand Forks Herald* (North Dakota), January 14, 2023. *The Untouchables* was one of many popular TV series produced by Desilu Productions.

50. *Reprisal!* (with an exclamation point added by the studio) was based upon the novel *Reprisal* by Arthur Gordon. The novel was set in Georgia during the post–World War II era and was about the lynching of an African American.

51. Daves, *Broken Arrow*.

52. Leah Candolin Cook, "The Last Apache 'Broncho': The Apache Outlaw in the Popular Imagination, 1886–2013" (MA thesis, University of New Mexico, 2014), 75.

53. Daves, *Broken Arrow*.

54. Arnold wrote that Jeffords "tried to make himself more of an Indian than the Indians themselves"; see *Blood Brother*, 356.

55. Cowans, in *Empire Films and the Crisis of Colonialism*, asserted that "*Broken Arrow* is not hostile to interracial marriage at all" (258) and that "Hollywood was generally well ahead of public opinion on this issue, and pro-miscegenation films vastly outnumbered films with frankly hostile outlooks" (270).

56. In 1956, the Motion Picture Association of America (now, the Motion Picture Association) revised the Production Code, removing any references to miscegenation. See *Variety*, September 15, 1954, 3, 16; August 25, 1954, 1; *Motion Picture Daily*, December 12, 1956, 6–7; and *Motion Picture Herald*, December 15, 1956, 13–15.

57. Cowans, *Empire Films and the Crisis of Colonialism*, appendix B, 349–53. Additionally, Cowans categorized fifty-three postwar movies as "mixed-race characters" that include the much-overlooked Martin Pawley (a Cherokee) and his union with a white woman in *The Searchers* (1956). Absent from Cowans's list is *Tulsa* (1949), which concludes with an interracial romance between a Cherokee rancher (Susan Hayward) and a non-Native heir to an oil field (Robert Preston).

58. See, for example, the interpretation of the Code in *The Film Daily*, December 20, 1931, 9, versus the *Motion Picture Herald*, August 11, 1934, 11. (Martin J. Quigley, co-author of the Production Code, was the publisher of the *Motion Picture Herald*.) Other publications, like the *Film Daily Year Book* (1944) and the *International Motion Picture Almanac* (1932, 1938) both clarified in their reproduction of the Code that only Black/white miscegenation was forbidden.

59. Robert M. W. Vogel, Letter to Joseph I. Breen (head of the Hays Office Production Code Administration), Motion Picture Association of America, AMPAS.

60. For an excellent discussion of differing policies toward Black/white versus Indian/white marriages, see Bethany R. Berger, "Red: Racism and the American Indian," *UCLA Law Review* 56, no. 591 (2009): 626–27, 633.

EPILOGUE

1. *Los Angeles Times*, April 26, 1956, 23.

2. *Colorado Springs Gazette-Telegraph*, August 22, 1969, 33.

3. Hollywood Chamber of Commerce, "Jay Silverheels Next Star in Hollywood Walk of Fame," *Press Release*, July 9, 1979. Silverheels's star is located at 6538 Hollywood Blvd.

4. Haes, "The Incarceration of the Chiricahua Apaches," 4–6, 11, 13, 16, 30, 41.

5. Robinson, *Apache Voices*, 58–59; and Deborah Antinori, "Chief Naiche: A Study in Complicated Culture Shock with Reactive Mourning and Depression," unpublished paper, 1991, Collection of H. Henrietta Stockel, Amerind Museum, 10–12, 13.

6. Antinori, "Chief Naiche," 13–14.

7. Naiche's biographical information is from "Naiche (Natchez) Public Profile," April 27, 2022, geni.com.

FURTHER READING

BOOKS

Aleiss, Angela. *Hollywood's Native Americans: Stories of Identity and Resistance.* Praeger, 2022.

———. *Making the White Man's Indian: Native Americans and Hollywood Movies*. Praeger, 2005.

Ball, Eve. *Indeh: An Apache Odyssey*. University of Oklahoma Press, 1980.

Canfield, Douglas J. *Mavericks on the Border: The Early Southwest in Historical Fiction and Film*. University Press of Kentucky, 2000.

Carter, Matthew, and Andrew Patrick Nelson, eds. *ReFocus: The Films of Delmer Daves*. Edinburgh University Press, 2016.

Corkin, Stanley. "Cold War Westerns and the Law of the Gun: *Broken Arrow* and *The Gunfighter*." In *Cowboys as Cold Warriors: The Western and U.S. History*. Temple University Press, 2004.

Cowans, Jon. *Empire Films and the Crisis of Colonialism, 1946–1959*. Johns Hopkins University Press, 2015.

———. *Film and Colonialism in the Sixties: The Anti-Colonialist Turn in the US, Britain, and France*. Routledge, 2018.

Frankel, Glenn. *High Noon: The Hollywood Blacklist and the Making of an American Classic*. Bloomsbury, 2017.

Hearne, Joanna. "The 'Ache for Home': Assimilation and Separatism in Anthony Mann's *Devil's Doorway*." In *Hollywood's West: The American

Frontier in Film, Television, & History, edited by Peter C. Rollins and John E. O'Connor. University Press of Kentucky, 2005.

Horlock, Douglas. *The Films of Delmer Daves: Visions of Progress in Mid-Twentieth-Century America*. University Press of Mississippi, 2022.

McNeill, Joe. *Arizona's Little Hollywood: Sedona and Northern Arizona's Forgotten Film History 1923–1973*. Northedge & Sons, 2010.

Neale, Steve. "Vanishing Americans: Racial and Ethnic Issues in the Interpretation and Context of Post-war 'Pro-Indian' Westerns." In *Back in the Saddle Again: New Essays on the Western*, edited by Edward Buscombe and Roberta Pearson. British Film Institute, 1998.

Rader, Dean. "*Broken Arrow*." In *Seeing Red: Hollywood's Pixeled Skins*, edited by LeAnne Howe, Harvey Markowitz, and Denise K. Cummings, 75–78. Michigan State University Press, 2013.

Smith, Jeff. *Film Criticism, the Cold War, and the Blacklist: Reading the Hollywood Reds*. University of California Press, 2014.

Smyth, J. E. "The New Western History in 1931: RKO and the Challenge of *Cimarron*." In *Hollywood's West: The American Frontier in Film, Television, and History*, edited by Peter C. Rollins and John E. O'Connor. University Press of Kentucky, 2005.

Walker, Michael. "The Westerns of Delmer Daves." In *The Book of Westerns*, edited by Ian Cameron and Douglas Pye, 123–160. Continuum, 1996.

ARTICLES

Aleiss, Angela. "A Brief History of Hollywood Honoring Native Talent." *Hollywood Reporter*, Awards Season Report, November 27, 2023.

———. "Hollywood Addresses Postwar Assimilation: Indian/White Attitudes in *Broken Arrow*." *American Indian Culture and Research Journal* 11, no. 1 (1987): 67–79.

———. "A Race Divided: The Indian Westerns of John Ford." *American Indian Culture and Research Journal* 18, no. 3 (1994): 167–86.

Arnold, Elliott. "Ceremony of the Big Wickiup." *Arizona Highways* 27 (August 1951): 8–15.

Ceplair, Larry. "Who Wrote What? A Tale of a Blacklisted Screenwriter and His Front." *Cinéaste* 18, no. 2 (1991): 18–21.

Cobos, Juan. "Una conversación con Delmer Daves." *Film Ideal,* 106 (October 1962): 612–17.

Foley, Tom. "Examining the Mythic Past: 1950 Westerns and Interdisciplinary Interpretation." *Concept: An Interdisciplinary Journal of Graduate Studies* (Villanova University), 36 (2013).

Fitzgerald, Michael Ray. "Evolutionary Stages of Minorities in the Mass Media: An Application of Clark's Model to American Indian Television Representations." *Howard Journal of Communications* 21, no. 4 (November 19, 2010): 367–84.

———. "Television Westerns, Termination, and Public Relations: An Analysis of the ABC Series *Broken Arrow,* 1956–1958." *Film & History: An Interdisciplinary Journal* 41, no. 1 (2011): 48–70.

Lahti, Janne. "Silver Screen Savages: Images of Apaches in Motion Pictures." *Journal of Arizona History* 54, no. 1 (Spring 2013): 51–84.

Lee, Susan Savage. "An Act of Redemption: Conflicting Images of American Indians in *Broken Arrow* and *The Searchers.*" *Journal of American Studies of Turkey* 48 (2018): 85–109.

Manchel, Frank. "Cultural Confusion: A Look Back at Delmar Daves' *Broken Arrow.*" *Film and History* 23 no. 1–4 (1995): 57–69.

Prats, Armando José. "His Master's Voice(over): Revisionist Ethos and Narrative Dependence from 'Broken Arrow' (1950) to 'Geronimo: An American Legend' (1993)." *ANQ: Quarterly Journal of Short Articles, Notes, and Reviews* 9, no. 3 (Summer, 1996): 15–29.

Seymour, Deni J. & George Robertson. "A Pledge of Peace: Evidence of the Cochise-Howard Treaty Campsite." *Historical Archeology* 42, no. 4 (2008): 154–79.

Taft, Joseph, ed. "Dialogues with a Director: Delmer Daves." *Persimmon Hill* 5, no. 2 (1975): 40–53.

Tavernier, Bertrand. "The Ethical Romantic." *Film Comment* 39, no. 1 (January–February 2003): 42–49.

Wicking, Christopher. "Interview with Delmer Daves." *Screen* 10, no. 4–5 (July/October 1969): 55–66.

THESES/DISSERTATIONS

Cook, L. Candolin. "The Last Apache 'Broncho': The Apache Outlaw in the Popular Imagination, 1886–2013." Master's thesis, University of New Mexico (Albuquerque), 2014.

Iglésias, Lauriane. "Le Patrimonialisation d'un Western Américain en France: Le Cas de *Broken Arrow*." In "La Flèche Brisée (1950) de Delmer Daves." Master's thesis, Université de Lyon, 2018.

Jansen, Pamela A. "Images of Native Americans in Film: The Cases of *Broken Arrow, Dances With Wolves*, and *Black Robe*." Master's thesis, University of North Dakota, 1995.

Jones, Elizabeth Pelletier. "Letters from the Blacklist: The Un-Friendship of Albert Maltz and Michael Blankfort." PhD diss., Boston University, 2017.

Jones, George Elwood. "The American Indian in the American Novel, 1875–1950." PhD diss., New York University, 1958.

Kvet, Bryan W. "Red and White on the Silver Screen: The Shifting Meaning and Use of American Indians in Hollywood Films from the 1930s to the 1970s." PhD diss, Kent State University, 2016.

Laluk, Nicholas C. "Historical-Period Apache Occupation of the Chiricahua Mountains in Southeastern Arizona: An Exercise in Collaboration." PhD diss, University of Arizona, 2015.

ARCHIVES

Albert Maltz Collection (#150), Howard Gotlieb Archival Research Center, Boston University

Albert Maltz Collection, American Heritage Center, University of Wyoming

Association of American Indian Affairs, Seeley G. Mudd Manuscript Library, Princeton University

Cecil B. DeMille Collections, Archives and Manuscripts, Harold B. Lee Library, Brigham Young University

Collection of H. Henrietta Stockel, Amerind Museum, Dragoon, AZ

Delmer Daves Papers (M192), Department of Special Collections, Stanford University Libraries

Gwen Bagni Papers, 1940–2001, UCLA Special Collections

Margaret Herrick Library, Academy of Motion Picture Arts and Sciences

Oral History Program at Columbia University: Popular Arts Project, Interview with Delmer Daves

Papers of Elliott Arnold, 1920–1980, University of Arizona Libraries Special Collections, Tucson

Twentieth Century-Fox Film Corporation, *Broken Arrow* Pressbook, New York Public Library at Lincoln Center

US Indian Census Rolls, 1885–1940

Warner Bros. Archives, USC Cinematic Arts Library